THE STUDY OF GOOD LETTERS

H. W. GARROD

From a pencil sketch by Sir Muirhead Bone

THE STUDY OF GOOD LETTERS

BY

H. W. GARROD

EDITED BY JOHN JONES

GREENWOOD PRESS, PUBLISHERS
WESTPORT, CONNECTICUT

Library of Congress Cataloging in Publication Data

Garrod, Heathcote William, 1878-1960.
The study of good letters.

Reprint of the ed. published by Clarendon Press, Oxford.
CONTENTS: The place of Hazlitt in English criticism.--Matthew Arnold as critic.--Tolstoy's theory of art. [etc.]
1. Literature--History and criticism--Addresses, essays, lectures. I. Title.
PN511.G3 1975 809 75-9845
ISBN 0-8371-8119-4

Originally published in 1963 by the Clarendon Press, Oxford

This reprint has been authorized by the Clarendon Press, Oxford

Reprinted in 1975 by Greenwood Press,
a division of Williamhouse-Regency Inc.

Library of Congress Catalog Card Number 75-9845

ISBN 0-8371-8119-4

Printed in the United States of America

'What I am trying to do is to advance the study of good letters'

ERASMUS, *Spongia*

'If there is a journalism of scholarship, he is its greatest practitioner'

H. W. GARROD

'Erasmus in Praise of England'

EDITOR'S NOTE

THERE are four things here which have not been printed before. 'Sir Henry Savile' is a lecture delivered in the Hall of Merton College on 30 November 1949, to mark the quatercentenary of Warden Savile's birth. 'Max and Merton College' is Garrod's contribution to a manuscript Birthday Book 'affectionately presented to Max by some of his friends and admirers on the occasion of his eightieth birthday'. Max was eighty in 1952, and his Book now lies in the Beerbohm Room in Merton. 'Thrillers' belongs to Garrod's time at Harvard (1929) as Charles Eliot Norton Professor of Poetry; it was read to a university society there. And soon after his return to Oxford, in November 1930, he reported his impressions of 'Fair Harvard' in a second paper, this one addressed to the undergraduate Bodley Club of Merton.

'The Place of Hazlitt in English Criticism' comes from *The Profession of Poetry* (1929); 'Matthew Arnold as Critic' from *Poetry and the Criticism of Life* (1931); 'Poetry and the Critical Art' from *The Study of Poetry* (1936); 'Dogs' from *Genius Loci* (1950). 'Tolstoy's Theory of Art' is the Oxford Taylorian Lecture of 1935. 'Housman: 1939' Garrod published in the learned journal *Essays and Studies* (vol. xxv, 1939). 'Oliver Goldsmith' stands as Introduction to a Selection of Goldsmith in the popular series Nelson's Poets (1924). 'Phalaris and Phalarism' is among the *Seventeenth*

Century Studies presented to Sir Herbert Grierson in 1938. The article 'Erasmus in Praise of England' appeared in *The Times Literary Supplement* of 11 July 1936. 'Reference-Books' is a clutch of five reviews: Bayle belonging to the *TLS* (24 April 1953) and the others to the *Oxford Magazine* (20 November 1941, 30 January 1941, 13 February 1941, 7 March 1946—in the order in which they are printed here).

I have taken many small liberties with Garrod's text, the least small being the omission of the first two pages of the Hazlitt lecture. Also in that lecture (p. 13; compare *The Profession of Poetry*, p. 104) 'general outline' is preferred to the Clarendon Press printer's 'genial outline'. One feels sure that the conjecture would have amused H. W. G., particularly if he had always intended 'genial'. Right or wrong, however, the credit must go to Mr. E. K. Willing-Denton who has been the active friend of this book throughout.

Permission to reprint 'Oliver Goldsmith' has been granted by Messrs. Thomas Nelson & Sons, and permission to reprint 'Erasmus in Praise of England' and 'Bayle and his Dictionary' by The Times Publishing Company.

CONTENTS

THE PLACE OF HAZLITT IN ENGLISH CRITICISM

When Hazlitt lay dying, something moved him to say that he had 'had a happy life'. So it pleased him strangely to sum up a sullen childhood, a youth moody and passionate, a manhood of which poverty, middle-aged erotics, and the self-torment of a temperament suspicious and morose, were the distinguishing characters. I think it likely enough, even so, that he knew what he was saying. His real life lay in literature, hidden there as in some passion of religious faith. After enumerating some of his favourite authors, 'To have lived', he writes, 'in the cultivation of an intimacy with such works, and to have familiarly relished such names, is not to have lived quite in vain.' I never read him without feeling that literature meant more to him than it means, not merely to common men, but to the other great critics.

His father was a nonconformist minister; and he destined his son for his own calling. But Hazlitt dissented from Dissent, as from everything else; and by nineteen he had had enough of being educated for that ministry. From nineteen to twenty-four he indulged the only educational experiment worth trying—self-education. For five years he sat at home, reading, marking, inwardly digesting—in the world's phrase, doing nothing. The five years, however, contained the great event of his life, his meeting with Coleridge. At five-and-twenty he turned painter; and at nine-and-twenty dropped painting for philosophy. Later he played with the theory of politics and with political economy; and he was thirty-eight before he found his true direction—the criticism of men and books. Yet I should not suppose his failures lost. If he never qualified for the dissenting ministry, at least the genius of dissent was with him through life. If he never learned to paint—to paint, that is, beyond a standard better than tolerable (and therefore, to so passionate a temperament, not tolerable at all)[1]—he may yet be conceived to have learned from painting some of the most characteristic effects of his writing. From his studies in philosophy, certainly, he carried over to the criticism of literature results which were vitalizing to his whole critical method. His first book was a philosophical essay, modestly, but cumbrously, entitled: *An Argument in favour of the Natural Disinterestedness of the Human Mind.* Whether the argument was a good one or not—philosophically—does not much matter; nor am I able to judge. What matters is that Hazlitt begins and ends in the conviction that men are, in fact, disinterested, and not selfish; a conviction real to him in a way that it hardly can be to a corrupt or venal temperament; a conviction which helped him in the interpretation of literature, particularly, I

[1] Yet his portrait of Lamb (in the National Portrait Gallery) is a notable picture. He painted Wordsworth, but destroyed the portrait—there was that in Wordsworth, he knew well, which—on canvas or in words—he could never quite hit. It would have been interesting to have his portrait of his father—'cracked and gone', he says of it, but 'as fine an old Nonconformist head as one could hope to see in these degenerate times'.

should suppose, in the interpretation of Shakespeare, whose greatest tragedies, if man be in his ultimate nature little, mean nothing. *The Characters of Shakespeare's Plays*—Hazlitt's first essay in literary criticism—was published in 1817, when, as I said, Hazlitt was already thirty-eight years of age. This has always been a popular book; and it would not be Hazlitt if it did not abound in fine thoughts finely expressed. None the less, of Hazlitt's purely literary works—and outside these it is beside my intention to stray—I conceive it to be the least satisfactory. All Shakespeare criticism is, in the nature of things, disappointing; and so far as Hazlitt can disappoint, he does so here. There is defect of knowledge, a thing which neither surprises nor offends me; but there is some defect also of courage. Hazlitt is doing what later he neither could nor would—he is holding himself in. But he liked the book himself, and, looking back on it, claimed that he had done 'more than any one except Schlegel' to 'vindicate the characters of Shakespeare's Plays from the stigma of French criticism'. A far better book is the *Lectures on the English Poets*, and better still—principally as being more courageous—the *Lectures on the English Comic Writers*—these belong respectively to the years 1818 and 1819.[1] Two years later came the lectures on the *Dramatic Literature of the Age of Queen Elizabeth*; and in 1825 *The Spirit of the Age*, followed, in the next year,

[1] In 1818 Hazlitt published *A View of the English Stage*: 'a collection of Theatrical Criticisms', written for various newspapers during the four years preceding. The book belongs rather to journalism than to literature; but contains much vigorous and characteristic writing. It is a good deal more like Hazlitt than the rather timid *Characters of Shakespeare's Plays*.

by *The Plain Speaker*.[1] This period, 1817–26, is Hazlitt's height of power. Within it fall, besides the books I have mentioned, *The Round Table* and *Table Talk*—essays on men and manners rather than upon books, but containing also much miscellaneous literary criticism—to the *Round Table* series, for example, belongs the admirable critique of Wordsworth's *Excursion*. *The Spirit of the Age*, published in 1825, had been begun, in fact, in December of 1823; and about half of it was finished in the first months of 1824. Dates are dull things; but these are worth remembering for the reason that this book, Hazlitt's best, is the product of the darkest period of his personal history. He had just been divorced from his wife; and he had just come through the sordid and unhappy love-affair of which he wrote, in *Liber Amoris*, an unashamed history. Add to this that his finances were desperate; and that his books, upon which he depended for his living, had been the subject of savage and unjust critical attack. They had been attacked, although, taken together, they constitute a body of literary criticism more vital than anything since Dryden. But neither fortune nor the malice of men could tame Hazlitt; and precisely from the period of his worst affliction springs his best work. From the experience of the man his work has taken, it would seem, a deeper dye of poetry—indeed, some tinge of tragedy. If he is still morose, yet he has discovered what we might have thought did not exist—the sublime of morosity.

Whether Hazlitt is the greatest of the English literary

[1] *The Plain Speaker* is a miscellany; but the best parts of it (some of them in Hazlitt's noblest style) are those which touch literature.

critics must depend upon the view you take of what literary criticism is or should be. If it is the business of literary criticism to criticize itself, to be chastened before it chastens, Hazlitt has no pretension to do this. He has many prejudices, and few reserves; he is sometimes mean, more often generous, rarely or never merely just. If it is the duty of the critic to separate the accidents of a literary work from its permanent effects, to isolate it, in analysing, from all possible contamination with interests and passions not completely relevant, to work upon it with no instruments of judgement not properly sterilized—this, and the like, lies outside Hazlitt's scope and care. Again, if the best criticism rests upon the best information, upon a wide acquaintance with literatures ancient and modern, upon scholarship and the comparative method, here too Hazlitt is defective—his reading is deep and not wide. Indeed, he is bold to affirm that 'our love for foreign literature is an acquired or rather an assumed taste . . . like a foreign religion adopted for the moment to answer a purpose or to please an idle humour'. If it is a part of criticism, once more, to formulate laws, to reach inductively general principles of literature, and to bring particular examples of prose or poetry before this court of principles, then the talent of Hazlitt is not more than a brilliant empiricism. Nor, when he can find no law, has he that instinct for adjournment which serves lesser men; he never wants to wait for posterity; of that higher court he entertains no apprehensions; he must get on with his business—a part of which is writing for his living and living by his writing. In a word, if the essential qualities of criticism are knowledge, patience, impartiality, analytic industry, stay of judgement—these are not Hazlitt's characteristic virtues; and in some of them he is more wanting than is proper either to genius or good sense. On the other hand, the defects which come from the excess of some of them it is a principal merit in him that he escapes. He is never, like Macaulay, a prig, nor a posterity-server. He does not, as Matthew Arnold does, just miss being a dandy of criticism; and he never, like Bagehot, commits the fault of philosophizing beyond what he can carry—of being deeper than he was dug.

His positive merits are numerous and palpable; indeed, I know no writer of such open excellencies, of excellencies so readily seizable and so delightfully handleable. First among them I should put, what seems not so much a talent of literature as an accidental grace of nature, his abounding *memory*. That sounds nothing much; but it all depends on what you remember, and how it is done. Of Hazlitt's memory, the principle is, not mental accuracy, but sentiment. No man ever quoted so much, and in no writer, I am afraid, will you find the same quantity of misquotation; as an advertisement for the Pelman Company, Hazlitt is no good at all. But it makes no difference—none, that is, if you take a free spirit freely. Macaulay draws upon a memory extraordinarily apt and accurate; he draws upon it—very impressively and deliberately. What is so delightful in Hazlitt is that he never *draws* upon memory at all. It all gushes, the spontaneity of it is never suspect; of themselves the springs of memory well up in inexhaustible freshness. Very often, as I say, the quotations are inaccurate; and very often they emerge, less their inverted commas, their patent marks effaced—just Hazlitt himself, the swift flash of his own prose. You must have plenty of the pedant in you to mind this. But it is easier to be a pedant than the unlearned believe; and there are not wanting people to tell you that this element in the style of Hazlitt bores them. Only bores are bored; and the truth is that this is neither an artifice nor an artlessness in Hazlitt's style, but the native resonance of his temperament. The great phrases of the great masters of speech were a part of his life, perhaps the part most real and effective; it was as natural for him to express himself in these as it is hard for other men to express themselves in any other terms than the meagre symbols of their individual crafts.

From this genius of sentimental memory flow a number of interesting consequences. As he grew older, Hazlitt wrote more and more, and read less;[1] and he is not the first man upon whom the need of feeding the body has imposed the necessity of scanting the soul. The late Professor Ker has observed, what once it is noted nobody can miss, that in his best writing Hazlitt is living on the spiritual riches of his youth. Of one or two other English writers, the same is true. The charm of Goldsmith, for example, hangs upon the sentiment of his years of vagabondage, his country youth and poverty. That gives him his tenderness, his lovable quality. Yet another example is Lamb. Of the first books which Hazlitt read, 'let me', he

[1] 'Books have in a great measure lost their power over me; nor can I revive the same interest in them as formerly' ('On Reading Old Books', *The Plain Speaker*, 1826).

cries, 'still recall them, that they may breathe fresh life into me, and that I may live that birthday of thought and romantic pleasure over again!' Hazlitt's best reading and thinking were done, not only when he was young, but when the new world-interests ushered in by the French Revolution were also young. Just as Goldsmith remains always a child, so Hazlitt remains always a young man. It is one thing to remember one's youth; another to keep it by doing so; and Hazlitt masters both accomplishments. His zest for greatness—revolutionary greatness above all—never leaves him; and to the end he retails fine actions, and still more great words, with unmatchable gusto. I do not mean that you will not find in him some at least of the qualities of middle years; in particular, the persuasion that men and things are not so good, or rather, not so great, as they were. With most of us that is what I call a conservative persuasion. But it takes Hazlitt differently: with him it is a devouring radicalism. If to be more radical at fifty, and with less excuse, than at twenty; to retain an unalterable conviction that the revolutionary dreams of youth are the only truths—if all that be conservatism, be middle-agedness, then middle-aged Hazlitt is, and a very Tory of the Tories. He is esteemed a rather sour writer; and certainly he is, in expression, sometimes a degree tart. He judges men and things by the standard of a too fretful righteousness. The age of which, in *The Spirit of the Age*, he essays to delineate the dominant characters, was an age, truly enough, of great men; but of great men all a little absurdly situated. For Hazlitt they were all of them renegades—or, what fretted him yet worse, the best of them were renegades—in that *best* was the sting. They were the apostates of that revolutionary freedom of which he was the Abdiel,

> faithful found
> Among the faithless, faithful only he,
> Among innumerable false, unmoved,
> Unshaken, unseduced, unterrified.

The just conviction of a mind unseduced by worldly interest makes him unjust to others. That Wordsworth should be an honest man and a distributor of stamps, that anything but the seduction of the world should have effected in Coleridge the shift from *Conciones ad Populum* to the *Lay Sermons*, in Southey that from *Wat Tyler* to *The Vision of Judgment*—all this appeared to him plainly incredible. Of Scott—who was at least consistent—he writes that he 'should be heartily glad if the greatest genius of the age should turn out to be an honest man'. He could kneel to Scott, he told Patmore, but he could not take his hand. Hunt comes within the same condemnation as Wordsworth and Coleridge:

> While my friend Leigh Hunt was writing the *Descent of Liberty*, and strewing the march of the Allied Sovereigns with flowers, I sat by the waters of Babylon and hung my harp upon the willows . . . while others bowed their heads to the image of the BEAST, I spit upon it and buffeted it and made mouths at it.

To these great men, therefore (whose situation was, really, not so much unintelligible as absurd), he is unjust. Yet unjust only to a certain point, and unjust always, I think, in a rather great fashion. Hear him upon Coleridge:

> I may say of him here, that he is the only person I ever knew who answered to the idea of a man of genius. He is the only person from whom I ever learned anything. There is only one thing[1] he could learn from me in return, but *that* he has not. He was the first poet I ever knew. His genius at that time had angelic wings, and fed on manna. He talked on for ever; and you wished him to talk on for ever. His thoughts did not seem to come with labour and effort; but as if borne on the gusts of genius, and as if the wings of his imagination lifted him from off his feet. His voice rolled on the air like the pealing organ, and its sound alone was the music of thought. His mind was clothed with wings; and raised on them, he lifted philosophy to heaven. In his descriptions, you then saw the progress of human happiness and liberty in bright and never-ending succession, like the steps of Jacob's ladder, with airy shapes ascending and descending, and with the voice of God at the top of the ladder. And shall I, who heard him then, listen to him now? Not I! . . . That spell is broke; that time is gone for ever; that voice is heard no more; but still the recollection comes rushing by, with thoughts of long-past years, and rings in my ear with never-dying sound.

To miss the merit of that is hardly possible. I do not suppose that Coleridge liked it—Coleridge who, when Hazlitt died, wrote upon him a mean satirical epigram. But it is unjust in the grand manner; and that manner mean spirits never compass. And, after all, it is unjust only to a part of Coleridge; and to a very real greatness in him

[1] He means common honesty.

splendidly just; while in its passionate faithfulness to a great memory there is characteristic pathos.

It is the same with Wordsworth. I do not think that Hazlitt was ever drawn towards Wordsworth in the same impelling fashion as towards Coleridge. Wordsworth's 'egotism', he says, 'is in some respects a madness. For he scorns even the admiration of himself, thinking it a presumption in anyone to suppose that he has taste or sense enough to understand him'. There is personal pique in that, I fancy; but neither personal pique nor political wrath affect seriously the substantial justice of Hazlitt's judgements upon Wordsworth's poetry. He girds, he carps, he jibes; but it never occurs to him to think of Wordsworth otherwise than as indisputably the first poet of his age, or to allow you to think that he thinks otherwise. Perhaps the only really bad critic is the critic who has learned, in Matthew Arnold's phrase, to 'praise what he despises and to disparage what he admires'. Never, or very rarely, I think, does Hazlitt do that. Spiteful and intemperate he often is; and that the minds and motives of men should be so cross-tracked and convoluted as they are irritated him. He had that conviction that all roads are straight which belongs to men who have never turned the corner of their youthful radicalism. But at least his judgement is never seduced by interest.

It is no small thing in a critic that he should keep always this unbribed judgement. Upon this Hazlitt prided himself, in a fashion more fussy, perhaps, than there was need; but not without title. The consciousness of his own disinterestedness brought with it the temptation to be perverse in his rectitude, to hunt opinions just because they were not those of other people. In a lesser man this would matter more. But not the least of Hazlitt's virtues is one which I have still to mention. The temptation to eccentricity was controlled by a natural truth of judgement, which he possessed in a degree not often equalled in the criticism of literature. Keats, who, if admirations must be mutual, had no particular reason to like Hazlitt, reckons as one of the three precious and incontestable realities of the time 'Hazlitt's depth of taste'. It is easy to forget, when enumerating the qualities of a great writer, some of the more obvious ones; it is easy to fly off in the praise of things about him not essential, easy not to remember that, in the long run, he is to be valued *for the truth of his opinions*. About Keats's phrase, 'depth of taste', I feel (quite apart from the confusion of metaphor which it involves) some difficulty. I do not feel that Hazlitt is properly to be thought of as a deep, or profound, writer. Yet upon the whole I conceive him to have a flair for truth in which no English critic rivals him; to have a quicker sense than any other for the difference between good and bad, between the genuine and tinsel. This he owes partly to the fact that his mind is *steeped* in good literature; and still more, I am inclined to think, to a fundamental genuineness in himself—a genuineness that all his faults are not enough to overlay. He really *is* disinterested—and not merely morally, but (what matters almost as much) intellectually—that is to say, he is unpedantic, for pedantry is only a want of intellectual disinterestedness, it is an interest in something other than the direct object of criticism. Hazlitt's flair for the truth is especially illustrated in his judgement of contemporaries. I know no critic who has placed so well the great writers of his own time. It is usually esteemed a difficult and delicate business; and perhaps Hazlitt is successful in it because he thought it neither. All his judgements are direct, unhesitating, unembarrassed; and most of them are right. At least they are right on the broad issues. Upon points of detail he is sometimes perverse; as when he prefers Byron's *Heaven and Earth*, of which the whole is rubbish, to *Don Juan*, of which the best is better than anything else in Byron. Yet he always knows who is who, even if he cannot always say unerringly what is what. He is better in general outline than in minute study. I think better of Byron than better critics do; but even here I am not outraged by, I find a substantial truth in, the sharp phrase in which Hazlitt tries to sum Byron's merits and defects, the 'sublime and provoking coxcomb of poetry'—there were two classes whom Hazlitt always hated, coxcombs and pedants. Even in detail, his judgements upon Byron, though he greatly underestimates his power in satire, flash often with fine penetration. What could be better, for example, than this, upon *Childe Harold*? The poem contains, Hazlitt writes, 'a lofty and impassioned review of the great events of history, of the mighty objects left as wrecks of time; but he dwells chiefly on what is familiar to the mind of every schoolboy; and has done no more than justice to the reader's preconceptions by the sustained force and brilliance of his style and imagery'. The last clause explains truly at least one-half of the immense vogue of Byron's poetry: Byron found the rhetoric for the romantic prejudices of his age; he is clothier and haberdasher to other people's preconceptions. That is only one side of him, of course; and he had affronted Hazlitt, it should perhaps be remembered, by blowing hot and cold about Napoleon. About Napoleon Hazlitt had a permanent kink in judgement. But what he says about Byron's 'preposterous liberalism' is not more, I think, than fair comment. With Byron's 'preposterous liberalism' he contrasts what he calls the 'gratuitous [i.e. unpaid, unbought] servility' of Scott—to the advantage of Scott, and still with some instinct for fairness and plausibility. The phrase 'gratuitous servility' is itself cleverly adjusted. Scott's poetry, it was easy to judge truly—easy, I mean, for Hazlitt—and he does not mind doing it. 'What is he to Spenser,' he cries, 'Spenser, over whose immortal ever-amiable verse beauty hovers and trembles?' There you have a criticism, not profound, but extraordinarily characteristic—bringing Scott into just that contrast in which he cannot live, and in just the words which diffuse the sense of what he is not. This contrasting eye is one of Hazlitt's great critical gifts. He uses it, not merely to put to you the difference between one great man and another, but, what is less easy, to illustrate how different this or that individual great man may be from himself, how antithetically mixed is any human greatness. To Scott's novels he is splendidly just—by no one are they better praised. 'The Author of *Waverley*, who has five hundred hearts beating in his bosom!'—that is fine amends for many slaps at 'Sir Walter' ('I have no liking to *Sir Walter*').

He may be accounted lucky in his time. For what a

gallery of telling personalities is *The Spirit of the Age*—to keep still to that work of Hazlitt by which he is best judged! He has hung there, it is true, one or two glaring portraits of nobodies—a thing which happens to all artists. Occasionally a figure is wanting which we miss—Keats, for example, or Shelley. Of his opinion of both Keats and Shelley he has given us scattered indications elsewhere; but neither here nor elsewhere a full-length portrait. He felt himself no longer young enough to enjoy the *Eve of St. Agnes*: 'but I know how I should have felt at one time'. He called Shelley a 'sophist'. One does not like it, but one can see what it is in Shelley that the phrase hits. Yet most of the interesting men of the time are in this book, and they are still interesting. If that is a merit in them, it is a merit also in Hazlitt. Many of them were bookish men, but in Hazlitt they are men, and not books. He valued books above all as the expression of human freedom, and in each and all of the persons he writes about what interests him is the relation in which they stand to the cause of human freedom. Thus he secures for them permanent connexions; and indeed, it was not in his nature to think of books in abstraction from the social and political life of man. He tended, it is true, to like books better than men; yet in books he was never quite happy until he had got down to the man in his habit as he lived. Upon the poetry of Wordsworth, he has made many fine critical observations; but we are grateful when he rounds them off with such a paragraph as this:

Mr. Wordsworth in his person is above the middle size, with marked features, and an air somewhat stately and

Quixotic. He reminds one of some of Holbein's heads, grave, saturnine, with a slight indication of sly humour, kept under by the manners of the age or by the pretensions of the person. He has a peculiar sweetness in his smile; and great depth and manliness and a rugged harmony in the tones of his voice. His manner of reading his own poetry is particularly imposing; and in his favourite passages his eye beams with preternatural lustre, and the meaning labours slowly up from his swelling breast. No one who has seen him at these moments could go away with an impression that he was a 'man of no mark or likelihood'.

These traits he likes to keep for us; partly, no doubt, because he was himself a painter before he was a writer; but still more, I think, because he was sensible that a book is but a part of a man, and that one of the plagues of literature, and of time, is that we lose the comment of personality. He is for ever pretending, of course, that it is not a plague but a blessing. But he does not convince even himself; and because he does not, he is a good critic. He never deals in ghosts or abstractions. He likes always flesh and blood and social environment, some touch of drama and its ironies. Indeed, he allows himself, I am afraid, to be too much preoccupied by the ironies. While it is his merit to see that a man and his book are a unity, he is too often too irritably sensible of the imperfect character of the unity; so that he comes to speak sometimes as though man and book were a kind of unworthy quarrel, or, indeed, the man a mere interruption to the book. He rounds upon and rails at the interruption. That personality and the expression of it should not fit, affronts him—and the more in proportion as circumstance had made his nature irritable and suspicious.

No word have I said of Hazlitt's style; and I have left myself time for very few words indeed. 'We are mighty fine fellows,' said Stevenson, 'but we cannot write like William Hazlitt.' The grand style Hazlitt has not; but of the *telling* style he is the consummate master. The method of his style is sweeping and hurried. He paints in broad slashes, caring little for subtlety in detail or for harmonization of effects. He is wrongly spoken of as an impressionist. There is a definiteness in the effects of his style, a certainty of outline, which is in no way impressionistic. His style has no mysteries, no seclusions of depth, no faint horizons: it never runs into distance. It is written in paragraphs but thought in sentences. It holds together, not by any natural unity of the thoughts, but by the astonishing swiftness of their succession. Telling stroke follows telling stroke so rapidly that there is no time to ask questions. Between the individual deliverances there is no bond of unity save that all are telling. I suppose that he should be called an epigrammatic writer. I suppose that it is an epigram when, for example, of the Rev. Mr. Irving—who took advantage of being a big man to pose as a great one—he says, 'Take a cubit from his stature, and his whole manner resolves itself into an impertinence'; or when he says of Mr. Gifford that 'he is admirably qualified for the situation which he has held for some years by a happy combination of defects, natural and acquired'; or even when he says of Sir Francis Burdett that 'he could not have uttered what he often did [in the House of Commons] if, besides his general respectability, he had not been a very honest, a very good-tempered, and a very good-looking, man'. For epigram, however, as a study in perfect expression, or as the art of saying what you think so concisely as to suggest that you do not think it, Hazlitt has no real aptitude. He has no real aptitude for it, firstly, because he is an honest man in a hurry; and secondly, because, as I have said, more than most men, he hated coxcombry and pedantry.

Will you bear with me still if I try to sum in half a dozen sentences a few of the merits in critical writing which I suppose myself to discover in Hazlitt? First, I would say, it is a good thing *not to be a dull writer*; I care little how it is managed, it is a good thing in itself. Secondly, it is a good thing to write about books as though they really meant something to you. It is a good thing, again, if you write about books, to be somebody—not to be somebody else, but to be individual, to make criticism reflect personality. It is a good thing, once more, even if you pay for it in prejudice, to know what you like and do not like. It is a still better thing—though this, again, is not a complete insurance against prejudice—to be disinterested. Best of all is it to have a natural flair for the truth, an eye for what is vital and vivifying. The first book to kindle Hazlitt's interest in literature was Burke's *Letter to a Noble Lord*. There, said Hazlitt, you have 'a man pouring out his mind on paper'. Just that praise is Hazlitt's own everywhere. To that praise you may add something further. For his writings as a whole, Hazlitt made in his last years the claim that, whatever their general merits, at least he had 'written no commonplace, and no line that licks the dust'.

That is a high claim for a man to make for himself who wrote always for his living. But it is, I think, a just claim; and because it is so, I should think Hazlitt, of all men who, in this kind, have written for their living, the most likely to live long.

MATTHEW ARNOLD AS CRITIC

I LAMENT the declined vogue of Matthew Arnold's critical writings. When I was young and clever he was the pattern of critical style and method. Today I do not observe that young men read him; though I do not detect in them, as compared with the generation which they have supplanted, any falling off either in the art of being clever or the science of being young. Even when I was young, let me add, he never appealed to Scotchmen. I never knew why. Lamb said that he had been trying all his life long to like Scotchmen. I knew Scotchmen who have tried hard to like Matthew Arnold; but none that ever made more than an indifferent success of it. It is not their want of humour. The most slashing attack upon Arnold's critical reputation which is anywhere to be found is in an essay by Walter Raleigh. Though a Scot, Raleigh had a quick and excellent humour. He was, moreover, as good a critic as we have had since Matthew Arnold himself. Like Matthew Arnold he was, in his best period, a professor in Oxford. Like Matthew Arnold, in the heart of him he despised Shelley; and they had other common sympathies. But Scotchmen do not like Matthew Arnold—and there is an end of the matter. In addition, Raleigh had a strong distaste for the saintly character. He was the son of a Scottish minister. Born in the manse, sermons and expressions of piety vexed him pitiably. In respect of Matthew Arnold, he could never rid himself of the feeling that the criticism of literature was being treated as though it were part of the Church service.

There *is* that in Matthew Arnold; and there were persons other than Scotchmen whom it irritated. Mr. T. S. Eliot, in a recent essay, has instituted an elaborate comparison between Matthew Arnold and F. H. Bradley. When he left Harvard, Mr. Eliot betook himself to an Oxford college where he was near neighbour to Bradley, and indeed, under one roof with him. It happened to be my own college; so that I wonder whether Mr. Eliot ever heard Bradley—as I heard him more than once—deliver his soul upon Matthew Arnold. I cannot think so; or he would not have supposed that the two men had much in common. Matthew Arnold was the first Professor of Poetry in Oxford who was a layman. He was not only a layman, but a somewhat unbelieving one. He held that 'miracles do not happen'. He did not believe in a personal God, nor in a personal immortality. Of Christ he supposed the distinguishing character to be his 'sweet reasonableness'—the kind of praise you might bestow on Sainte-Beuve. But the heart of him, even so, was priestly. In his last years he used to attend the chapel services at Harrow School. He was probably the only unbeliever in the congregation. But alone of the congregation he always insisted on turning to the east at the Creed. And this High-Church ceremonial manner he carried into literature; there is too much turning to the east in his criticism. Bradley hated Matthew Arnold's High-Church manner; and he hated still more the Low-Church morality, or moralism, that accompanied it.

I recall the contempt with which he used to speak of Matthew Arnold's lecture on Heine; he had heard Arnold deliver it—and it is certainly a rather incompetent performance. All this would never have happened to Heine (you feel) if, at the proper age, *he had been confirmed.* I like to think that Mr. Eliot—so modern as he is (or was till yesterday)—reads Matthew Arnold. But Bradley had no patience with him; and is just so much like him as any one Oxford man is like another—and no more. It was an unlucky parallel. Mr. Eliot essays, if I remember rightly, some comparison of the literary styles of the two men—but, again, with wasted ingenuity. The two styles stand contrasted as the pointed and the diffused. I doubt if Matthew Arnold ever wrote a *pointed* sentence—or Bradley any other kind of sentence. I have a liking for epigram—I were a prig else; but Matthew Arnold starves me of it. Matthew Arnold is a great stylist who never made an epigram. Bradley is an epigrammatist who never made a great style. Both writers indulge, often, an ironic manner. But how different they are, even here: Arnold seeking his divine pattern in Plato, Bradley a little earthy in his dependence upon Gibbon and Voltaire.

But I mentioned Bradley and Mr. Eliot only to indicate a certain sympathy which I have with those persons who are offended by what may be called the priestly and the moralistic elements in Matthew Arnold's criticism. I say 'a certain sympathy'; for I am not prepared to carry it too far. I admit a tendency in Matthew Arnold to call no man a poet until he has been baptized and confirmed. He too much liked decorum, literary and moral. He preached too much, using too often the same texts. A man can have but one excuse for preaching—a religion. Matthew Arnold's religion was poetry—those of us who are so happy as to have better ones are, I suppose, the better for it. In the collapse of the creeds, Matthew Arnold took what he could get. 'There is not a creed which is not shaken,' he writes, 'not an accredited dogma which is not shown to be questionable, not a received tradition which does not threaten to dissolve . . . most of what now passes with us for religion and philosophy will be replaced by poetry.' Of whatsoever things are spiritual he supposed the greater part to be found in poetry. Deeply impressed by the consolations of poetry, he supposed the truths of it to illustrate life, attaching immense importance to moral truth. His dictum that poetry is a criticism of life I have never felt to be absurd, but it can easily be made to seem so.

The absurd things that critics say live after them; and even of their gay half-truths the saving qualifications commonly perish with them. Matthew Arnold has the ill luck to be best remembered by a travesty of his views on the relation between poetry and moral ideas, and by one or two bad misfires of critical judgement. His judgements upon French poetry I leave aside. But he preferred Shelley's letters to his poetry; he thought Byron a better poet than either Shelley or Keats or Coleridge. Worse than that, he wanted the feeling for Burns; and yet worse, he was unable to appreciate Chaucer. These judgements are perhaps less remarkable than the method by which they are reached. This may be called the method of the *Frogs*, the method which furnishes such admirable fooling in Aristophanes' comedy of that name. In effect, it consists in selling poetry by the pound. Aristophanes takes a pair of scales. Into the one scale he throws a number of lines of Aeschylus, and into the other a number of lines of Euripides. The better poetry consists of the lines which weigh heavier; the light stuff is the cheap stuff. For the accuracy of the scales you have to take the word of the critic. Matthew Arnold operates this method, not like Aristophanes, with partial seriousness and partial honesty, but really trying to be honest with it and succeeding in being serious. The method may be seen in its most elaborate employment in his essay upon *The Study of Poetry*. There he takes (*inter alia*) a line of Dante, a line of Chaucer, and—rather unfairly, but not meaning to be unfair—two lines of Milton. He likes Chaucer's line (as you knew he would) the least of all. That might proceed from the circumstance that he misquotes it. But no! That you may not doubt his perfect impartiality, he misquotes, you will find, all three authors. Having done that, he assures you gravely that there is nothing like carrying with you everywhere, in your head or your heart, the great lines of the great poets, and trying out against them the little lines of the little ones. From the great lines you will get to know the 'grand style'.

However, even here Matthew Arnold achieved something. He set people talking about the 'grand style'. He had made a phrase. 'You can still influence people,' Disraeli said to him, 'for you can still make phrases.' That has perhaps some touch of cynicism—else it were not Disraeli. 'The world is still ruled by names', Gibbon had said, long before. It is hateful, of course, that a writer should live by purveying catchwords; and it is painful to feel that one belongs to a public taken in by the way things are said. We tell ourselves accordingly that nothing is so precarious as the life of a catchword, and that literature is something better than phrase-making. So it is; but even so I marvel at the life-saving quality of good phrases—how often, at our great moral crises, they come unsummoned, messengers of salvation to weary and despondent souls. And indeed, if the theory of style means anything, the matter of a good phrase is some truth, or, what is sometimes more wanted, some half-truth. Some of Matthew Arnold's distinctive phrases—the 'grand style', 'high seriousness', 'the free play of ideas', 'sweetness and light', 'the best that has been known and thought in the world'—these, I suppose, even today, when they have forfeited their vogue, enjoy repute. It is easy to speak of them as a kind of advertising captions; and of Arnold as a singularly successful advertising agent for 'Ideas'. But after all, ideas are not soap and cigarettes; and the truth is that with these phrases of his Matthew Arnold did succeed in interesting an immense public in the subjects his phrases summarize. It is perhaps good enough wit, and certainly cheap enough, to speak of him as 'travelling in sweetness and light'. That is, even so, a sweet and light-bringing occupation. I suppose it might be said of Carlyle that he travelled in moral righteousness; or of Dr. Johnson that he travelled in good sense. The truth is that we all travel, but most of us get nowhere, and few of us deliver the goods.

Be this as it may, Arnold's phrases had, while he lived, an immense and widely operative vogue. In the vogue that they had, perhaps he took too much pleasure. Yet he never troubled to make his phrases too striking. Some of them are hardly phrases at all. Most of them carry only just so much of phrase as to serve the purpose for which they were invented. The quality of them is, indeed, not so much striking as caressive and flattering. And generally: I know no other great writer who so much flatters the vanity of his readers; each of whom, as he reads, is sustained by the constant sense that he is acquiring sweetness and light and that he is one of a very few persons who are doing so. I suppose that the Athenian sophists used similar arts of flattery, caressing men into culture, and that that is a part of what Plato objects against them. Just so much a sophist I will concede Matthew Arnold to be; and it must, I suppose, be accounted a kind of baseness to make men love knowledge for the good conceit of themselves which goes with it. But in a deeper sense, I will not agree that Matthew Arnold is a sophist—though unsophisticated persons have called him one. If I conceive rightly his aim in criticism, it was the exact opposite of that of the sophists. For the crime of the sophists was precisely this; that they taught an interested love of knowledge. They taught, not a pure interest in ideas, but a love of ideas essentially related to practice, to politics, to party. The range of Matthew Arnold's interests was wide. Leave aside his defect of history—which is patent—and forget his contempt for science; not merely in literature, but in education, in politics, in religion, he was deeply interested and well informed. Literature was, I suppose, his first love; but if he had stayed there, he would not have been, I am inclined to think, a better critic than some others. It is precisely the interest which he had in education, politics, and religion which makes his criticism original. The value of literature lay, he supposed, in its power to furnish a temper of mind; to create that disinterested habit of intellect which secures for ideas a free play. Education, politics, religion, are immensely important subjects; to bring to them, not the prepossessions of pedantry, nor party spirit, nor fanaticism—all of which proceed from either ignorance or narrowness—but to set playing on these subjects minds habituated to free or liberal motions, minds nursed on ideas, minds informed by the best that has been known and thought among men—that is what is everywhere wanted, this is that soul's salvation which literature, and literature only, can work out in us. Of all that Matthew Arnold says upon Criticism that is the main substance. It is said with the most plainness and vigour in the first of the *Essays in Criticism*; but all the other essays say it again, or they say nothing. Something like it, of course, is said by other critics; something like it is said whenever the claim of ideas is pressed against the tyranny of any materialism. But the energy and bright persuasiveness with which Matthew Arnold urges his cause, the skill of temper which he lends to his plea, the variety with which he illustrates his single thesis—these things make him original.

The study of literature ends in a disposition of mind; its best gift to us is some faculty of spiritual freedom, a certain largeness of temper. No one, perhaps,—not even the mere aesthetician—will be much disposed to quarrel with that.

But Matthew Arnold goes somewhat further than that. He valued literature, I think, just in proportion as it creates the temper in which to view the great interests of life. In this he is not quite consistent with himself. Sometimes, for example, he seems to think of poetry as though its first business were to furnish anodynes for life. Occasionally, he concedes to it some rather sober power of joy. Very rarely, perhaps never in his heart, does he think of it as a pure source of pleasure, a delight among other delights. In the main, as I say, he values literature for the temper which it teaches—poetry a temper of heart, prose a temper of the intellect; in either kind, the temper for looking at the great interests of life. For Matthew Arnold the great interests of life are the social and political and the religious. I think we too much forget how strong the obsession was with him, not merely of the religious interest, but of politics and the theory of society. Often enough, I know, he runs from politics—even from religion—to the consolations of poetry. Yet more often you might suppose him interested in literature only for its power to fit a man to judge questions of religion and social life. Indeed, if I am to mark him off as a critic from other critics, to find that in him which is individual, I can best do it, I think, by saying that beyond any other man of letters he valued the temper of the man of letters—conceiving it, not as an end in itself, but as an instrument of the art of living.

Of the temper of the man of letters he is himself, I must think, the fullest embodiment that our literature can show. I am bold to call Hazlitt the first of English critics, giving him a place which many people, perhaps most, would suppose to belong to Matthew Arnold. I stand to what I say the more cheerfully that I think it possible to find first places for both my favourites. I am satisfied to call Matthew Arnold our greatest man of letters; and I add to that, what sounds a paradox but is none, that he is a man of letters who became a literary critic by accident. We are so used to thinking of him as a critic of literature, of poetry especially (and as a literary critic he achieved work of such distinction), that we too easily forget how casual in fact were his connexions with this province. They were casual, intermittent, and in some respects not wholly congenial. If we leave aside a book which was published posthumously, the second series of *Essays in Criticism*,[1] Arnold has to his credit, in the department of literary criticism, only two books, one good, one bad. The good one is the *Lectures on Homer*; I think it may still pass for his masterpiece; and it was, in fact, his first book of criticism. The bad one—though it is impudent to christen so a book everywhere charmingly written, and full of interesting and stimulating criticism—is *The Study of Celtic Literature*. Matthew Arnold did not know enough about his subject; and generally not enough was known about the subject. The book remains, with all its merits, a rather useless performance. Neither of these books had any success—neither the good one nor the bad one: neither of them was reprinted during Arnold's lifetime. Both had, of course, an Oxford vogue—a thing which to a good many persons seems worse than no vogue at all. The Homer book was the first-fruits of Arnold's

[1] The different essays had been written, for the most part, between 1879 and 1888, and had appeared in literary periodicals.

Oxford professorship; a professorship to which he had been elected, not because he was a critic, but because he was a poet. He was not a critic—he had written no criticism at all. In prose, he had to his credit a political pamphlet (now a bibliographical rarity) and two blue books—official publications of the Education Commission; one of these blue books he made into a real book. He took his blue books always with great seriousness. What is more, they interested and influenced a wide public—one or two of them, re-shaped into what I call real books, had a wider circulation than any of his purely literary works. Education, politics, religion—these, really (after poetry, which he abandoned very early), were his primary interest; these, and not the pure criticism of literature. Save for the accident of the Oxford professorship, I am not sure that it was in his heart to be a literary critic at all, as that phrase is most naturally understood. Certainly, he put his heart into the Homer lectures; but the *Celtic Literature* is a little perfunctory—it was a part of a task, with not much more than curiosity behind it. Nor for the most part was Arnold's public interested in him as a literary critic. He first found himself, and the public first found him, and became interested in him, when he published the first series of the *Essays in Criticism*. Perhaps one-half of that book—or less—may be regarded as pure literary criticism. But already the religious interest is seen obtruding itself—in some of the essays inappositely. The best essays are those which indulge social, or politico-social, criticism. Of the literary essays not one, unless it be that on Heine, is concerned (save parenthetically) with a writer of the first class—the best of them is that on Maurice de Guérin; and of that the principal charm derives from Arnold's delicate touch in biography.

This book was followed three years later (1867) by *Culture and Anarchy*—plainly called, this, in its title-page 'An Essay in Political and Social Criticism'. Political and social criticism was what the public wanted; and the book sold. I do not mean that it had an extravagant success on the Book Club scale. But while there was no demand at all for Arnold's purely literary essays, *Culture and Anarchy* and the first *Essays in Criticism* went through several editions. In style and manner *Culture and Anarchy* may, in any case, rank with Arnold's best work. I may notice that, though it was an essay in social and political theory, much of it had formed the substance of lectures delivered from the Oxford Chair of Poetry—a circumstance that may serve to indicate how roomy that chair is.

But all the while that Arnold was thus mixing politics with poetics, he was moving towards a more dangerous occupation than either—theology. It has been found convenient to forget that it was by his theological writings that he first rose into the rank, or esteem, of a great writer. His first piece of pure theology was *St. Paul and Protestantism*—published in 1870. I have the fancy that of all his books this is, in some ways, the best written. Three years later appeared *Literature and Dogma*. I hate to reckon literary greatness by publishers' sales. But while Arnold's best book, the *Homer* Lectures, was, as I said, never reprinted in its author's lifetime, and while even his second-best book, the *Essays in Criticism*, took four years to reach a second edition, *Literature and Dogma* went through four editions in its first twelve months. Man is a political animal, says Aristotle. He is in some degree also a poetical one, though he rarely shows it. But above all, he is a theological one; and he shows it whenever you give him the chance.

A successful writer upon educational, political, and theological subjects—who had once written poetry which nobody read, and who from time to time wrote literary criticism which not very many people read—that, I think, would be a fair description of Matthew Arnold as he appeared to his contemporaries. In the last decade of his life he permitted editors and publishers to wring from him now and again a purely literary essay—perhaps a dozen such essays fall within this period; the best of them are the six that stand first in the posthumous second series of *Essays in Criticism*. But they are casual and accidental glories—the by-products of a talent primarily interested in something else.

It is important to get this perspective. It is odd how often the world cares to remember us only by our by-products. Wisdom is no doubt justified of all her children; but she makes her best success very often of the illegitimate ones. Most of the questions in which Arnold was interested no longer interest anybody. His theological writings are, save so far as he is our only artist in theology, no longer vital. When he first wrote on education, there was none—it is perhaps not his fault if there is now too much. How changed the face is of politics and society, I need not say; if there is any real break in the continuity of English political history, it falls between Arnold and ourselves, and not at the Rebellion or the Revolution. To questions of politics and society Arnold brought a strong antipatriotic bias, which has ceased now to be irritating—who today thinks of preferring his own country to other people's? Upon all these subjects, however, Arnold was an extraordinarily effective writer. In connexion with them his writings will always be documents historically interesting; and, a hundred years hence, will seem perhaps more important than they are—from their pervasive readability and from their temper, the temper of a man of letters consistently looking at the world in the manner which literature has taught him.

For us, these merits have become not much more than interesting adjuncts to Arnold's proper fame, his fame as a critic of literature. As a critic of literature I rate him, after all deductions made, very high. Some of the deductions that have to be made I have already hinted, and others are obvious. I am not prepared to break my heart over the fact that he is not what is called a scientific critic. I am not offended by the circumstance that he not only shows no interest in, but in fact deprecates the use of, the historical method—the master-discovery of his age. I am not offended by it; nor surprised at it; for the truth is that Arnold was not a learned man—that was why he sometimes talked as though he knew everything. He knew very little about the history of literature, and he liked to think (what may be true) that great poetry drops from the skies. In general, he indulged too much the appeal to absolute standards. He can as little tolerate that criticism should be personal as that it should be historical; and he loses a good deal here in warmth and colour. It is a habit of great poets, i.e. romantic poets, to seem not to belong to the world of books—to seem out of keeping with the serenities and decorums of literature. Expatiating in the Sacred Grove of poetry, Arnold hated to see human faces peeping out at him from behind the leaves—you could never tell when human nature, or the poetic nature, was not going to be malign, or even disreputable. Even so, he is not always consistent with himself; and in fact some of his best sketches are those in which the element of biography finds a place.

It is in a different way, I think, that Arnold disappoints us most. He concerns himself too much with the uses of literature, and too little with its pleasures. He attaches too much importance to taste, and too little to relish. By the waters of Helicon he sits down and sips, sampling them with the meticulous satisfaction of the wine-taster. It is horrible to see him, sometimes, tasting without swallowing. Nor in general has he, in appreciation, what I may call a good social manner. His criticism is tainted with a certain snobbery and even dandyism. All that is a defect, none the less, of a very real quality in him—he did believe in the best, and he did know that the best was not the shoddy. Most of us do not; really, most critics do not. Arnold's genuine flair for the best, the insistency of his faith in the best, his pleasant manner of sharing it only with the best men—a secret between you and him—these are first-rate virtues; and not the less effective for an element which they have of the *stagy*. For there *is* a good deal of the *poseur* in him—I not only concede it cheerfully, but, to be honest, I enjoy it. I like the good art of it, and the supercilious airy amiability with which it is managed. If Arnold carried into political and social criticism the manner of a man of letters, he also carried into the criticism of literature—or liked to think that he did—the air of a man of the world. The role afforded him artistic delight; and on the whole it was well suited to him. The part of it which he carries least well is the cosmopolitan pose, the affectation of being born on the Continent. But in general his bland finish of manner, and the delicacy of his irony, are beyond praise. If he is not the greatest of English critics, his make-up of being so is itself a piece of greatness; and not to enjoy it is a piece of stupidity.

Indeed, Arnold's real distinction, and the best hope for him of a permanent fame in criticism, is that he is so extraordinarily enjoyable. He is enjoyable almost everywhere; and a part of the enjoyment is, if we are honest with ourselves, the delight which we derive from a finely adjusted pose. I am not sure that we have not too much outgrown what I would call the simpler pleasures of literature—it is part and parcel of a general sophistication. But I will not be put off by it. Because others are sophisticated, I am not going to be ashamed to say that, after the fashion of the period in which I was born, I value literature very largely by the enjoyment which I derive from it. I am delighted in Arnold by what I feel to be the pervasive charm of his temper—it is not the less charming to me from the affectations that go with it. The style of mind, the manner, delights me—as an artistic product it delights me. And yet again, and finally, and yet more in the fashion of yesterday,

I enjoy above all things Arnold's beautiful English. Here again, some affectations that I am aware of do not hurt me —I think they enhance my satisfactions. Perhaps Arnold's style a little lacks masculinity; at least the he-men of literature do not write like this. Yet it has qualities which we shall be hard put to it to match in any others of our prose-writers. For a like delicacy of prose-style, for a prose equally characterized by symmetry and proportion and harmony, we are driven to French literature or to the ancient Greek. I hate to speak of truth of style—it opens the floodgates for bad metaphysic or for cant. But, properly guarded, the phrase does mean something. In Arnold's beautiful English I seem to myself always to find both grace and truth. Grace and truth are qualities rare, I suppose, in any age. Our own age wants grace perhaps more than truth. We *have* a kind of ugly truthfulness. But we too little esteem grace—and we have ceased to read Matthew Arnold.

TOLSTOY'S THEORY OF ART

A YOUNGER contemporary of Matthew Arnold, and a correspondent of Bernard Shaw, Tolstoy seems coeval, rather, with Lear or Melchizedek or Moses. In two particulars, certainly, he was more modern than Moses, but even so an anachronism. He had reduced the Ten Commandments to five; and he represented the last attempt upon earth to live according to the Sermon on the Mount. Moses had said, 'Thou shalt not kill.' Anuchin asked Tolstoy, 'May I kill a wolf that attacks me?' 'No,' said Tolstoy, 'if we may kill a wolf, we may also kill a dog, and then a man, and there will be no stopping.' He faced the consequences of the Sermon on the Mount in a spirit almost equally uncompromising. If he had not completely divested himself of property, he had come as near to doing so as a man can who is afraid of his wife. The last enemy to be overcome was copyright. The copyright in Tolstoy's works was a valuable property; and the tragedy of his last days turned on his confused endeavours to shed this property. In the end he made a will, which continued to be the subject of litigation until the Bolshevik Government included copyright in their general confiscation of property.

One of Tolstoy's correspondents, Verigin, who claimed (*inter alia*) to be the Messiah, regarded Tolstoy's Christianity as only partial. He pressed two points against him. It was all very well, he urged, for Tolstoy to divest himself of property. But why did he not divest himself of clothes? 'One must admit', he wrote, 'that even Christ and the Apostles were not able, all at once, to go naked.' But of Tolstoy he seemed to hope better things. Tolstoy, however, stuck to his peasant's coat and peasant's boots—the latter he made himself, and there seems to be no doubt that they were the worst-made boots in the world. Verigin's other point went in deeper. The writing and printing of books, he urged, is in itself sinful. Not only are books more often bad than good—a proposition no one will dispute—but the production of them involves an expense of human labour which ought properly to be devoted to creating food and shelter. Tolstoy had said things rather like this himself; but that did not oblige him to take them when said by someone else in slightly different language; and he goes so far as to call Verigin's argument a 'peculiarly sectarian contention'. But the barb stuck; and it is precisely in the endeavour to answer this 'sectarian contention' that Tolstoy's writings upon art have their origin.

It has been objected to the *Kreutzer Sonata* that it is a condemnation of marriage, and a plea for absolute chastity, written by a man who, after a libertine youth, had married and begotten thirteen children. I do not know that there is any answer except that we must take the saints as we find them. They often make it difficult for us. Tolstoy kept a diary of his youthful immoralities, a comprehensive book: when he married, he made his wife a present of it; and she read it diligently with tears. He was not yet a saint; but he was so far in danger of becoming one that he was utterly honest and had no sense of humour.

It would not be true to say that he began to write about art when he had ceased to be an artist; for to the period of his theorizings upon art belong both the *Kreutzer Sonata* and *Resurrection*, to say nothing of *Master and Man* and *Hadji Murad*. Yet his situation was paradoxical. He had put off the lusts of the flesh—though now and then they distressed him by unpredictable and unwelcome homecomings. So far as lay with himself, he had divested himself of property. But he had not put off art; the habit of which, even in second-rate natures, seems stronger, often, than any lust of the flesh or of riches. He had not put off art; and, as a saint and an honest man, he was obliged to ask himself why. Nowhere in the Sermon on the Mount was it said, 'Blessed are the artistic', or that the clever should inherit the earth. After all, who *were* the artistic? They were the upper classes; a ninety-nine per cent. aristocracy with a one per cent. solution of under-dog. Most of them were neither poor in spirit nor pure in heart; and instead of seeing God, they devoured widows' houses—they absorbed, that is to say, 'the intense and unwilling labour of thousands and thousands' occupied in the production of their books and instruments, their libraries, galleries, theatres.

Tolstoy had not yet put off art. That he was an artist was, when he began to write about art, almost his only contact with the world; and a part of his purpose was to justify that contact to himself. *What is Art?* is written partly for his own conscience, and belongs to the department of confessional literature. Nor was he a man who confessed by halves. 'I consign', he writes, 'all my own artistic productions to the category of bad art, except *God sees the Truth* and *A Prisoner of the Caucasus*.' In its prodigality of self-abnegation that rivals the Epilogue to the *Canterbury Tales*. Yet it is interesting to note that Tolstoy condemns his own writings, not—as Chaucer the *Canterbury Tales*—because they are 'sownen into sin', not because they are bad morality, but because they are bad art. And in general it is worth remarking that the bad morality of a book never shocked him. As regards literature 'sownen into sin', Tolstoy brought to the study of it the settled equanimity of a man who had examined his own heart and lived in Moscow. Here particularly he disconcerted his critics, writing about books like a man of the world, long after he had ceased to belong to the world. The truth is that to the problem of the place of art in human life Tolstoy brought prepossessions which were not primarily moral—far rather, the dominating prepossession is political and economic. By the moral badness of art his withers were unwrung; he was not shocked. But he was shocked, and profoundly, first by the appalling expensiveness of all art, and secondly by its privilege, its exclusiveness—like wealth, it had passed into the control of the upper classes. From its privilege, its upper-class character, followed the badness of the greater part of it, a badness in respect of which it was hardly worth while to distinguish between moral and artistic. 'Is it true', Tolstoy asks, 'that art is so good and so important an affair as to redeem all this evil?' Or is there not a 'terrible probability' that 'while sacrifices of the lives and labour of men, and of morality itself, are being made to art, art may be not only useless but harmful'?

This is the prime question of *What is Art?* Tolstoy

answers it with the good sense with which he so often surprises us. Art is a condition of human life. Without it, we should be, not men, but beasts. It is a means of intercourse, one of two principal means. By words we transmit thoughts, by art we transmit feelings. Art is 'a means of union among men, joining them together in the same feelings and indispensable for the life and progress towards well-being of individuals and of humanity'. I have no quarrel with that; though I would say that a man might vindicate government in terms little different. Equally with art government seems to be 'a means of union among men . . . indispensable for the progress towards well-being of individuals and of humanity'—only Tolstoy happens to love art and to hate government. He does not love art, I may notice in passing, because it is lovely. To explain art in terms of beauty is, he says, like explaining food in terms of its palatableness—the end of food is, not to please, but to feed. If, in addition to eating our food, we like it, that is, I suppose, just God's mercy—or the naughtiness of our hearts. Certainly, out of the naughtiness of our hearts Tolstoy explains our addiction to beauty. Beauty, he is bold to say, 'is at the root of our passions', and is 'contrary to goodness'. Speculations which identify the beautiful with the Idea, merging it in God, he dismisses as 'mystical', 'fantastic', 'founded on nothing'. From the temptation to connect art with beauty he was saved, it is worth remembering, by an accident of the Russian language, which, while it allowed an educated Russian to speak of a beautiful man or horse or house or landscape, made it unintelligible if he spoke of a beautiful poem or a beautiful piece of music or a beautiful action. That art often treats the ugly, or treats as ugly what is beautiful, is a reflection which, I think, did not interest Tolstoy.

On his final definition of art Tolstoy spent infinite pains. He defined art as 'a human activity consisting in this, that one man consciously, by means of certain external signs,[1] hands on to others feelings he has lived through, and that others are infected by these feelings and also experience them'. Of this definition—or rather of an abbreviated form of it[2]—Bernard Shaw says simply, 'It is the simple truth: the moment it is uttered, whoever is really conversant with art recognizes in it the voice of the master.' I do not think it is as simple as that. Many persons, for example, whom we must in fairness recognize as 'conversant with art' will not accept, what is central in Tolstoy's definition of it, the conception of art as a conscious communication. They will prefer to believe that art lies in self-expression; the artist expresses himself; and for himself; he is not concerned to ring anyone up on the telephone about it. But for Tolstoy art is essentially an other-seeking activity—the artist 'consciously' hands on feelings to others; and what he means by 'consciously' Tolstoy is careful to explain. 'Art begins', he says, 'when one person with the object of joining another or others to himself in one and the same feeling expresses that feeling by certain external indications.' I cannot think, again, that Shaw has stopped to ask himself just what Tolstoy means by feeling; but to this I shall come back.

[1] These 'external signs' are 'movements, lines, colours, sounds, or forms expressed in words'.

[2] 'An activity by means of which one man, having experienced a feeling, intentionally transmits it to another.'

In Tolstoy's definition the grand surprise is that it appears to exclude from the judgement of art all ethical considerations. The artist 'hands on' to others 'the feelings that he has himself lived through'. Using a metaphor not too happy, but selected with care, Tolstoy speaks of him as 'infecting' others with those feelings. I say 'selected with care' because, behind Tolstoy's choice of this metaphor, lies his conviction that three-fourths of modern art is no better than a disease. He believes that, and he is unwilling to forget it or to allow us to forget it. But equally he believes that art does not cease to be art by becoming a disease—provided only that the disease be infectious. The feelings that a man has lived through will be determined, it is obvious, by the kind of life he has lived; and in this or that artist they may be such as to constitute a body of disease impressive in its extension and complexity. But, for art, what matters is not the disease, but the presence or absence of infective power. The greater part of modern art is disease. But in proportion to its power to infect others, it is not less, but more, art.

This position Tolstoy states in terms plain and unmistakable. 'If a work', he writes, 'is a good work of art, then the feeling expressed by the artist—be it moral or immoral—transmits itself to other people', *infects* other people. 'The sole measure of excellence in art is the degree of infection. The stronger the infection, the better is the art, as art, speaking of it now apart from its subject-matter, that is, not considering the value of the feelings it transmits.'

All this is full of comfort—the most modern of us may sleep safe in his bed. But Tolstoy is, I have said, about as modern as Moses; and we ask ourselves, is there no trap? Shaw, when *What is Art?* first appeared, called the whole of it 'a most effective booby-trap', a booby-trap being, as I suppose, a trap laid by a simple-minded man to catch clever ones. But really simple-minded men—and Tolstoy had arrived at a simplicity of mind more staggering than any duplicity—really simple-minded men do not set booby-traps. He believed, quite simply, that the determinant of art is, not subject-matter, but form: he believed that so simply that he never asks himself, nor guesses that ever anyone else has asked, whether form and matter are not perhaps a single and indissociable effect. The determinant of art is, not subject-matter, but form. A work of art, as such, is not affected by the excellence or inferiority of the feelings it conveys: it suffices that it conveys feeling. What is the matter with Baudelaire and Verlaine, and the sixteen other French poets whom Tolstoy lists in his celebrated tenth chapter—together with 142 whom he could name, he says, if he saw fit—what is the matter with all of them is, not that they are bad men conveying bad feelings, but that they are bad men conveying no feelings at all, or conveying feelings obscurely—with an obscurity no whit redeemed by the circumstance that it is sometimes designed. That feeling belongs to a region of the soul in its nature obscure, seems never to occur to Tolstoy. It is the business of poetry, he says, to convey feelings; but of poetry which he dislikes it is the business, you might suppose, to *state* feelings, or even to convey thoughts. Mallarmé had said, 'To name an object is to take away three-quarters of the joy of the poem —which consists in the happiness of divining, little by little. To suggest, that makes the dream of poetry.' The sentence may contain exaggeration (I do not know that it does); but it is not nonsense. But for Tolstoy it has only to be quoted to be seen to be nonsense. It is at least better nonsense than saying that poetry must be as plain as a pikestaff.

Tolstoy does not say quite that. But having so defined art as to allow a place in the sun to the Decadents and Symbolists, he is determined that very few of them shall occupy it. He does not exclude them from the kingdom of art; but he makes the eye of his critical needle so thin that hardly the most emaciated of these camels has much chance to get through. That their subject-matter is immoral is not a crime of art; but it is a crime of art that they are unintelligible.

At any rate, they are unintelligible to the lower classes. That Mallarmé, say, may be intelligible to the intelligentsia, but unintelligible to the peasant, is a consideration which neither escapes Tolstoy nor disconcerts him. For the judge of art is not some Aristotelian *phronimos*, he is not the intelligent man; he is in fact the peasant. That seems absurd: and when St. Paul tells us that God chose the fools of the world, that too seems absurd—only we do not say so.

That Tolstoy, who had the courage of his religious convictions, should also have the courage of his aesthetic convictions is tiresome for no better reason, perhaps, than that suggested by Shaw—art is fashionable among us, and Christianity is not. It would be a mistake, however, to suppose that Tolstoy reached his aesthetic by way of his evangelicalism. Not only is that not true, but the contrary is true. That the judge of art was the peasant, and that God chose the fools of the world, was a discovery which he made long before he became a Christian; it was this discovery that led him to discover Christianity. He made the discovery between the years 1859 and 1862—nearly twenty years before his conversion, and nearly forty years before he completed *What is Art?* He made it when he was teaching school at Yasnaya Polyana; when Semka and Fedka—two peasant boy pupils—were writing for his school magazine stories which he has called 'equal to anything in Russian literature'. He was already then famous by his books; and it seemed to him, he says, 'strange and offensive' that he should be 'hardly able except at some happy moment to keep up with' these inspired peasant boys.

I do not know whether Tolstoy's theories of education—theories grounded in radical and bold experiment—have received proper attention from our professors of educational theory. I do not know what a student in this university reads, when he reads for the Diploma in Education. But I am pretty sure that he might do worse than read Tolstoy. Tolstoy's theory of art is, in any case, the just measure of his experience in education. When he set up his school for serfs in 1859, the question which he asked himself was, can good literature be made intelligible to the lower classes? When, thirty-eight years later, he wrote *What is Art?*, the question which he asked was, can literature be called good which is not intelligible to the lower classes? This later question he answers by bold negative.

Semka and Fedka are, no doubt, exceptional—like Burns,

they are peasants of genius. But Tolstoy does not stop at Semka and Fedka. 'Any peasant,' he says, 'any peasant of unperverted taste' can as easily distinguish good art from bad as 'an animal of unspoiled scent' can follow the trail. By 'a peasant of unperverted taste' he means plainly, as Shaw understood him, 'almost any peasant'; and Mr. Maude's criticism of Shaw is not better than trifling. Tolstoy, says Maude, 'is not speaking of the mass of the peasantry, but of a not very common individual . . . whose natural qualities have not been perverted by spurious art or otherwise'. In that case, he is saying of the peasant what would be equally true of the nobleman, and in respect of either tautologous. Equally with the peasant the nobleman of unperverted taste will have a good taste in art; and the true judges of art will be the few: in a single sentence Tolstoy will have denied what he wrote a whole book to prove. For peasants of unperverted taste, let us substitute the poor and simple. The poor and simple judge art more surely than the critics for a simple and single reason—they are the greater part of mankind. 'To say of a work of art', Tolstoy writes, 'that it is good, but incomprehensible to the majority of mankind, is like saying of a food that it is good but that most people cannot eat it.' Deeply influenced from his earliest youth by Rousseau, he believed that the greater part of mankind was good—so far as it was allowed to be by that small part of it which is bad, the part representing wealth and government. It was morally good—for art, an irrelevant consideration. But it was also artistically good, responsive to feeling, to feeling as conveyed by the forms of art. Relieved of those confusions of mind begotten in them by government and privilege, the many judge truly both life and art.

Good literature—at any rate the best literature—is what seems good to the many: the greatest literary happiness of the greatest number. The judgement of art rests ultimately upon a count of heads—or perhaps it would be truer to say, a count of hearts. The position has paradoxical consequences; the most obvious of which would seem to be that the best art is the art of producing best-sellers.[1] But Tolstoy bore a spirit undismayed by paradox. If he could sell the Sermon on the Mount at a penny, he was convinced that it would be a best-seller. He actually tried the experiment. But he had reckoned without the censor, who obliged him to excise the more objectionable passages. Clearly, upon one point he and the censor were in agreement—the Sermon on the Mount was intelligible to the lower classes.

They had indeed another point of agreement. Both wished the lower classes to have literature which was good for them—by which I mean morally good. Tolstoy excluded from the judgement of art moral considerations, and in what he says in this connexion he is, as always, perfectly honest. Like a good many Puritans, he hated prudery—to the degree that, in discussing the relations of the sexes, he employed often a vernacular which shocked modest persons. In general, again, he judged gently the

[1] I cannot satisfy myself that Tolstoy made much allowance for the time-element. His count of heads is in a different order from Dr. Johnson's appeal to the common sense of all time ('by the common sense of readers uncorrupted with literary prejudices, after all the refinements of subtlety and the dogmatism of learning, must be *finally* decided all claim to poetical honours').

sins of the flesh; and in his judgement of fleshly art and literature, formally heavy though it sometimes is, I seem to myself to detect the same charity—a charity neatly compounded of the gospel and the world.[1] He had persuaded himself, in any case, that the harm done by immoral art is, in the main, inconsiderable. A large part of it he dismisses—we have seen—as unintelligible. It is unintelligible from defect of form. The region of form he is not interested to explore otherwise than in a very general fashion—we have to content ourselves with knowing that there is a little more and a little less in technique which makes good or bad art. 'Art', said Bryulov, 'begins where the wee bit begins'; and there Tolstoy leaves us. If we ask how the artist achieves that 'fine snail-horn perception' of the little more and the little less which is the essence of art, which dictates form, he achieves it, we are told, by feeling. What determines form is feeling. For truth, or adequacy, of form, it does not require that feeling should be moral, but that it should be sincere. Lecherous feeling will do well enough, but requires its own sincerity. If the Decadents and Symbolists fail in art, it is because they first fail of sincerity. Most of them are insincere for a reason the most obvious in the world—they have the misfortune to belong to the upper classes—they have never dwelt with realities, they are copyists and *poseurs*.

Others of them, we might argue, are insincere for a different, and nobler, reason; and indeed from a kind of sincerity. The sincerity of the artist Tolstoy defines in

[1] He brings a much less degree of charity to books which glorify nationalism, arms, the Church, and privilege generally.

terms not ethical—all that is required of the artist is that he shall *really* love or hate what he describes. But so much being required, he must pay dearly for the divorce of morality from art—he must become what he acts, he must be as bad as his book. It is the salvation of art that this is not easy. Art is 'a human activity', and to love the bad is hard. How often does it not happen to the most modern of artists that, just when he thinks, good easy man, his decadence is a-ripening, some importunate humanity in himself plucks him back, giving to his art an indecisive character?

The determinant of art is, not content, but form. We take that and are thankful—only to discover presently that an almost constant concomitant of immoral content is unintelligible form. I say 'almost constant'. I think it has not been sufficiently noticed that of the three arts which principally interested him, poetry, music, and the art of the novel, the last—the art which he himself practised—received from Tolstoy what may be called a preferential treatment. In respect of poetry and music, it was easy for him to call unintelligible any work of which the content was morally unsatisfactory. But brought down to prose, to the novel, this was not so easy. In Maupassant, for example, he was confronted by an author who, beyond question, was 'master of a beautiful style, expressing what he wanted to say clearly, simply, and with charm'. It was no good saying that Maupassant was unintelligible. It could be said plausibly of Baudelaire, plausibly and perhaps even truly of Mallarmé. But said of Maupassant it was neither true nor plausible. If there had been no arts but poetry and music, I think Tolstoy would have felt more comfortable about his definition of art. But he was pulled up by prose. Cold prose convinced him that there could be such a thing as immoral art. But outside prose, outside the novel, it is remarkable how clean a sweep he is able to make of so-called works of art of which the content is ethically bad.

That the immoral novel exists, and that some examples of it must pass for art, seems common sense; and Tolstoy lets it go at that. It does not much help him that the appeal of Maupassant is limited.[1] For if his definition of art means anything, it means that any novel which succeeds in conveying immoral feelings is art—the sole measure of art is the degree of infection. Is art *really* as easy as all that—the possession of any dirty rogue?

The truth is that nothing in the world is easier than by means of words—or, for that matter, of picture post-cards—to convey immoral feelings, to infect others with our own obscenity. It is easy to be a dirty rogue, and not easy to be a Maupassant. Art begins, not when any dirty rogue communicates dirty feelings, but when an artist communicates artistic feelings.

To say so much, and to leave it at that, is, of course, to define art in terms of itself. And often, in the presence of some supreme example of art, we feel that there is nothing else to be done—it suffices to lift up hands of ineffectual wonder. In Tolstoy the element of wonder was deficient.

[1] It is limited by the fact that his subject-matter is unfamiliar and without appeal to the many, at any rate to the peasant. This does not affect the quality of his art, but its importance. That the peasant judges the *quality* of art truly because he is pure in heart and sees God, Tolstoy nowhere says, nor, consistently with himself, could say; but it is this in the peasant which makes him judge truly the *importance* of any work of art.

Not only does he nowhere explore the nature of artistic feeling, but everywhere he plainly denies its existence: the very conception of it is too airy and aristocratic for him. For him the feeling excited by a work of art is of the same class as any other feeling. With the froward poet you feel froward, but not with any transmuted frowardness. The sorrowing poet infects you with his sorrow, but he does not so temper it that it reaches you 'like a solemn joy'. The end of art is not to transmute feelings, but to share them. The feelings which art communicates are plain, straight, democratic.

When I began my examination of Tolstoy's definition of art, I expressed a doubt whether some of his interpreters had examined the terms of it with sufficient rigour. It was not in Tolstoy's heart, I have said, to lay booby-traps. Yet when art is said to communicate feeling, the one phrase contains, I think, two booby-traps, not the less formidable for being innocently laid. First, the feeling which the artist communicates is not special or aristocratic; it is not artistic—its only art consisting in the fact that it *has* been conveyed or communicated. It is the due or normal feeling excited by the object described, though some of us, of course, see and feel objects better and more truly than others. Secondly, art is defined in terms of its final cause, human intercommunication. Can such a definition be said wholly to exclude ethical considerations? The artist 'consciously' hands on to others feelings he has himself experienced. That means, I have said, that he does so with the object of joining others to himself. Art begins with the desire in the artist for union with others—a desire in itself of ethical character. It ends when that union is accomplished. But the condition of its accomplishment is a desire in those affected by art to be united both with the artist and with one another. Tolstoy does not make that explicit, perhaps, in his definition. But it is explicit in the context in which he sets his definition, and implicit in all his thinking. It is important that we should not miss it. I will content myself here with a single decisive sentence: 'However poetic, realistic, striking, or interesting, a work may be,' he writes, 'it is not a work of art if it does not evoke that feeling (quite distinct from all other feelings) of joy and spiritual union with another (the author) and with others (those who are also infected with it).' The social justification of art belongs to its essence. It is 'a means of union among men', a part of the service of universal love.

Is this to exclude ethical considerations? Is it not, rather, to open the flood-gates? There floods in, not only ethics, but politics. Art appears as a disguised socialism—that its best practitioners are the lower classes follows naturally.

I have been occupied for the most part with exposition, exposition mainly critical. Tolstoy issues from it, I am sensible, more naïve than I wished: partly from faulty adjustment of emphasis, but more because I have not had time to indicate those elements in *What is Art?* which I think permanently valuable. Let me mention only one aspect of it which makes it an admirable tract for the times. It sustains a magnificent fire of destructive criticism against a class of literary and artistic persons of whom every age has a few—and our own very many: those, I mean, who live by not being understood, or by creating the bad taste which makes them intelligible to one another. And everywhere the book is interesting and lively, everywhere it has that searching and heroical quality which characterizes all Tolstoy's best work, and which belonged to his life.

HOUSMAN: 1939

THE mortal men to whose discretion Housman committed the half of his immortality—the poems, that is to say, which he had not thought worth publishing—have now completed their task. The discharge of it began, in 1936, with *More Poems*; most of them better poems than *Last Poems*, even if less well punctuated. In the year following came *A.E.H.*, giving us eighteen Additional Poems, with a light garnish of letters and biography, to say nothing of a packet of nonsense verse. Of the eighteen poems none, perhaps, was unworthy; and three at least may rank with Housman's best successes. The nonsense verse also was well worth having—who had believed, else, that Housman had it in him either to be happy or to write nonsense? That many of the letters were worth having, I must take leave to doubt. The biographical sketch was revealing; perhaps it revealed too much.

And now there is nothing more to come, no more to let out. The *Collected Poems* of 1939 complete the Housman canon, furnishing an effective rejoinder to recent detraction. Collected and canonized, Housman waits now only the scholiast, and that 'academic appreciation which is the second death'.

Born in 1859 (with every opportunity, accordingly, of being a perfectly good Victorian), Housman was bred in High Anglicanism: 'much the best religion I have ever known', he calls it, rather impertinently—there was no 'Christian nonsense' about it, he explains elsewhere. But, like a greater poet, he was early corrupted by Lemprière's *Classical Dictionary*. This book, he writes, 'which fell into my hands when I was eight, attached my affections to paganism'. A pagan at eight, 'I became', he goes on to say, 'a deist at 15, and an atheist at 21'. This is very young talk, though it comes from his late years, when he knew, I suppose, what a deist was. He remained an atheist his life long, and was annoyed if anyone suggested that he was a mere agnostic. 'I wrote verse', he says, 'at eight or earlier [about the time, that is, of the lapse into paganism], but very little until I was 35.'

'There were occasions when memory played him false', writes Laurence Housman. But that he wrote very little poetry till he was thirty-five seems to be both true and verifiable. As an undergraduate he competed, unsuccessfully, for the Newdigate; and to the same early period belong two of his published poems—one of them, 'New Year's Eve', is full of first-rate stolen fire:

Oh, thou that seest our sorrow,
  It fares with us even thus:
Today we are gods, tomorrow
  Hell have mercy on us . . .

We are come to the end appointed
  With sands not many to run;
Divinities disanointed
  And kings whose kingdom is done . . .

But apart from these three undergraduate pieces, Laurence Housman was unable to find 'any trace of a poem earlier in date than 1890'. To that year belongs 'The Merry Guide'; of the three-and-sixty poems of *A Shropshire Lad* the first in time, the finest in tune, the most amiable in temper.

A Shropshire Lad, after being refused by Macmillans, was printed by Kegan Paul in 1896, in an edition of 500 copies, at the author's costs. There were 500 copies, I recall, of the original *Lyrical Ballads*; but of that celebrated undertaking the costs were borne by the publisher. Neither *Lyrical Ballads* nor *A Shropshire Lad* can be said to have sold like wildfire. Of either book it took two years to sell 500 copies. *A Shropshire Lad* was well praised, *Lyrical Ballads* had been roundly abused; so that a man might vainly wonder whether it pays better to be well or ill spoken of in the critical journals. Wordsworth and Coleridge were sufficiently paid in the intense regard of a small class of men to whom poetry was a religion. Housman's public was a good deal more miscellaneous. We were living, be it remembered, in that singularly harmless period, 'the nineties'. The king of naughtiness was Kipling; and Mr. Blackett, who managed Kegan Paul, knew very well what he was about when he designed for the *Shropshire Lad* a jacket showing rampant 'a yokel in a smock frock with a bunch of recruiting-sergeants' ribbons in his hat'. There was Kipling; and to Kipling *A Shropshire Lad* owed perhaps one-half of its early vogue. A less obvious influence (less obvious, I mean, to those coming after) was Stevenson. Laurence Housman, reading *A Shropshire Lad* for the first time, was moved to remark that it was 'better than Stevenson's *Underwoods*'. Recording the remark in his *A.E.H.*, he finds it necessary to remind the reader that Stevenson was then 'very much more in the fashion than he is now'. Housman's naturalism is studied out of Stevenson. But he had no use for half-measures; and, when Meredith called the *Shropshire Lad* 'an orgy of naturalism', it was not without provocation. Lecturing on Housman more than ten years ago, I called attention to the influence of Stevenson, not only upon Housman and the epigoni of Housman, but upon 'modern' poetry generally. Humbert Wolfe has more recently said something on the subject. And now, last but one in the *Collected Poems*, we have the lines 'R. L. S.', which Housman wrote in 1894. I do not know that he has anywhere else hinted his debt to Stevenson. I had suggested that some part of the likeness between him and Stevenson might be explained by that interest which both of them had in some French poets. Housman has since said that he had interested himself 'very little' in either Villon or Verlaine; and that the most obvious influences upon his poetry had been Shakespeare's Songs, the Scottish Border Ballads, and Heine. At least he shared with Stevenson an interest in Latin poetry and in Matthew Arnold. How much Stevenson learned from the Latin poets, Martial in particular, and from Matthew Arnold, was, I think, hardly guessed until his *New Poems* appeared posthumously. Nor till I read *A.E.H.* did I know how high in our poetry Housman set Matthew Arnold.

Of the occasions of *A Shropshire Lad* Housman has given his own account. I am not sure that he has not given two accounts, in some degree discrepant. In the prefatory note to *Last Poems* he speaks of the earlier book as written under the condition of a 'continuous excitement', a condition so overmastering that, should it ever return, the writer could not 'well support it'. I supposed that to mean, when I read it, that the poems of *A Shropshire Lad* were written in, and from, the passion or emotions which they treat. I found it (I said at the time)[1] 'interesting, because it has not been the way of some great poets. It was not the way of Byron, who speaks of his poetry as the language of his *sleeping* passions—when his passions were awake, the poetry in him died, he tells us. It was not the way of Wordsworth. Wordsworth's way was Byron's way; he had to set some interval between his emotion and the expression of it.' However, 'we must take poets as we find them', I added. Unhappily, we do not always find them the same yesterday and today. Housman has since given an account not easily harmonized with that of his Note. 'I did not', he wrote to a correspondent, 'begin to write poetry in earnest until the really emotional part of my life was over; and my poetry, so far as I could make out, sprang chiefly from physical conditions, such as a relaxed sore throat during my most prolific period, the first five months of 1895.' In a conversation with Sir Sydney Cockerell[2] he said much the same in his last years; explaining *A Shropshire Lad* as the product, in part of ill health, in part of a reaction from some quarrel over a point of classical scholarship.

All this may be true; but it does not make sense—least of all in conjunction with what is said in the prefatory note to *Last Poems*. Yet presently Housman made a theory of it, and wrote round it his celebrated lecture on *The Name and Nature of Poetry*. In that lecture the seat of poetry is, he

[1] *The Profession of Poetry*, p. 222.
[2] See *The Times Literary Supplement*, 7 Nov. 1936.

tells us in effect, the pit of the stomach; and 'Kipling says that I am "dead right" about the pit of the stomach', he records with evident satisfaction. There *is*, no doubt, something in the pit of the stomach; and others—Housman was not the first—have looked to physiology and pathology to explain genius and virtue. It seems still permissible to believe that the soul is not the body, and that we are poets only out of some spiritual experience. Without something happening to Housman at some time, and in some nobler part of him than the pit of the stomach, we should be without *A Shropshire Lad*. I may quote here, harmlessly, Laurence Housman: 'The astonished exclamation', he writes, 'of a member of the family, after reading the first six or seven of the *Shropshire Lad* poems, "Alfred has a heart!", is sufficient indication of the pains he had taken to conceal it [his heart] during the years of his bitter disappointment over the finish of his university career.'[1]

That Alfred's heart bore no wounds of the conventional kind, that he was never in love, that he was, indeed, what his brother calls him, 'a born bachelor', we must now, I think, take as certain. The cloud of witness seems convincing. Anyone whom it fails to convince might do worse than turn to page 41 of *The Name and Nature of Poetry*:

> Even Shakespeare, who had so much to say, would sometimes pour out his loveliest poetry in saying nothing.
>
> Take O take those lips away
>   That so sweetly were forsworn,
> And those eyes, the break of day,
>   Lights that do mislead the morn;

[1] *A.E.H.*, p. 75.

But my kisses bring again,
bring again,
Seals of love, but seal'd in vain,
seal'd in vain.

That is nonsense, but it is ravishing poetry.

To call that nonsense is to be, surely, not merely a 'born bachelor', but an old and crusty one. Not only is it not nonsense, but every line of it has its clear meaning, the whole of it as truly pure logic as it is pure poetry.

If 'Alfred had a heart', and not merely the pit of a stomach, what was he doing, we must ask, that his family did not find it out till he was five-and-thirty? Laurence Housman is surely right. He was hiding it. He had been hiding it ever since 'his bitter disappointment over the finish of his university career'. It is a lame, and even ludicrous, conclusion; that a man should hide his heart—hide it all his life long—because he had broken it over a 'plough in Greats'. The 'plough' happened in 1881. There followed an obscure chapter which Laurence Housman entitles 'The Heavy Change'—he does not attempt to penetrate the obscurity of it, because, during most of it, Housman 'was keeping his family at a distance'. He 'lay down in London' in what his brother calls 'proud seclusion', nursing, first in Bayswater, later in Highgate, immedicable wounds. Suddenly, in 1896, there fell upon the family the portent of *A Shropshire Lad*; and 'Alfred', they cried (or one of them cried), 'Alfred has a heart'. Alfred protested that he had nothing but a sore throat; and God help him, he could no other—for how could a man confess even to his family that he had a heart broken by a 'plough' in his schools, fifteen long years ago?

Does this seem trivial, and even ignoble? Was this all that had happened to him? At least it is all that can be verified; and if it were all that had happened *in* him, trivial and ignoble it would certainly seem and be. But by this entrance he had gone down into hell; and it is easier (says Virgil) to go down than to come up again. *Sed revocare gradum....* Nor, if a man emerges, can we expect him to be properly coherent. Once *down*, Housman had lived through, I do not doubt, one by one, all the themes of *A Shropshire Lad*. For we only write as deep as we live; and that book was not written but out of grim depth and hardness. If he had been crossed in love, everybody, I suppose, would think it all right. As it is, many people, and probably all Americans, have a feeling that they have been let down. It is as though you sought to explain Hamlet to them out of some early episode of his years at Wittenberg. 'But what, in faith, make you from Wittenberg?' For myself, having lived in a university continuously for more than forty years, I believe that I should understand Hamlet passably well if I had met him in his early student period. Right away, I should guess that what brought him to Elsinore was, not his father's funeral, but his own. Housman's perfectly real tragedy becomes, I feel, not less but more tragic from its inadequate occasion. For could anything, when all is said and done, be more properly tragic than this long disaster of a life and temperament selfish, morbid, inhumane, having its causes in a *hamartia* hardly falling within moral condemnation at all?

Of Housman's darkest period, the early years in London, I have noted already that very little is known. It is only known certainly that, whatever unhappiness there was, there were no unhappy loves. I have sometimes wondered whether there were no unhappy friendships. I have no wish to ask questions impertinently intimate. But one or two things, said and not said, in *A.E.H.* set me wondering; and then, in *Additional Poems*, I fell upon this:[1]

> He would not stay for me; and who can wonder?
> He would not stay for me to stand and gaze.
> I shook his hand and tore my heart in sunder
> And went with half my life about my ways.

Nor can anyone, I imagine, have failed to notice that it is the 'lads' of *A Shropshire Lad*, and not its 'lasses', that come in for the best of Housman's tenderness. In the days when that book had more devotees than it has now, I do not recall that I ever saw a woman or girl reading it. But 'lads' lost in it were plentiful as blackberries. I have heard it maintained, again, that Housman's 'best piece of poetry' is, not any of the poems of *Collected Poems*, but the set of Latin verses prefixed to his edition of Manilius. That is not more than good paradox; but the verses, even so, could have been written only by a man who had a genius for friendship. In friendship, too, did Housman's genius some time meet disaster?

The greater part of *A Shropshire Lad* was written in 1895. So were four poems of *Last Poems*. Of two of these four (so good are they) I could have guessed the date. One of them[2]

[1] It should be read in conjunction with 'Shake hands, we shall never be friends . . .', 'Oh, were he and I . . .', 'Ask me no more . . .', and perhaps xxii and xxxi of *More Poems*.

[2] 'Begun 1895, finished 1905.'

is 'In midnights of November. . .'. In the other, of three stanzas only, I suppose him to be addressing the Spirit of Superstition; but he liked poetry free of commitments:

Her strong enchantments failing,
  Her towers of fear in wreck,
Her limbecks dried of poisons
  And the knife at her neck,

The Queen of air and darkness
  Begins to shrill and cry,
'O young man, O my slayer,
  Tomorrow you shall die'.

O Queen of air and darkness,
  I think 'tis truth you say,
And I shall die tomorrow;
  But you will die today.

To 1896 belongs 'The chestnut casts his flambeaux', but the last stanza—and the best line,

The troubles of our proud and angry dust,

comes from 1922. Of the other pieces in *Last Poems* for which we have a date, something under a dozen come (substantially) from 1922. Most of the rest belong to the period 1899–1905; a rather weary aftermath of *A Shropshire Lad.* Of these poems of the aftermath I doubt if more than two ('The fairies break their lances...' and 'Oh stay at home...') were worth the mower's toil; and I marvel that so late as 1922 Housman cared to print such jaded Kiplingese as 'The Queen she sent to look for me . . . '. The glory of *Last Poems* is, of course, the 'Epitaph on an Army of Mercenaries', written in 1914, the inspiration of it fetched, I must believe, from some nobler source than a relaxed throat. I wonder, even so, whether it is so great a poem as another epitaph which Housman wrote for a later army:

Here dead lie we, because we did not choose
  To live and shame the land from which we sprung.
Life, to be sure, is nothing much to lose;
  But young men think it is, and we were young.

That is from the posthumous volume, *More Poems*:

ἐντάφιον δὲ τοιοῦτον οὔτ' εὐρὼς
οὔθ' ὁ πανδαμάτωρ ἀμαυρώσει χρόνος.

In their purity, tenderness, and simplicity, those four lines are Simonidean; and better—for Simonides used a sounding and coloured vocabulary, while here every word is ordinary and every word but two a monosyllable. *More Poems*, indeed, has more poetry, I think, than *Last Poems*. We have dates for two only of its pieces; the one belongs to the *annus mirabilis*, 1895, the other is 'For my Funeral' (1925). The latter piece was actually used, I think, at Housman's funeral service. For the memorial to him in Ludlow church an inspired friend selected the first three lines of another poem from *More Poems*:

Good-night; ensured release,
Imperishable peace,
  Have these for yours,
While sea abides, and land,
And earth's foundations stand,
  And heaven endures.

When earth's foundations flee,
Nor sky nor land nor sea
  At all is found,
Content you, let them burn:
It is not your concern;
  Sleep on, sleep sound.

Morere, Diagora! When a man can write like that, it is time to die; mortality cannot offer him further heights. We are not told when the verses were written; if the fifth and seventh lines recall to us the 'Epitaph on an Army of Mercenaries', they are not necessarily later. There are a dozen poems of *More Poems* which I should rank with the best successes of *A Shropshire Lad*; and the best of *A Shropshire Lad* I have never underrated—whole poems of it I have carried in my head and heart since I first read it nearly forty years back. I suspect, I almost think that I know, that of the dozen pieces I speak of very few are much later than 1895.

Ho, everyone that thirsteth
  And hath the price to give,
Come to the stolen waters,
  Drink, and your soul shall live.

Come to the stolen waters,
  And leap the guarded pale,
And pull the flower in season
  Before desire shall fail.

It shall not last for ever,
  No more than earth and skies;
But he that drinks in season
  Shall live before he dies.

June suns, you cannot store them
  To warm the winter's cold,
The lad that hopes for heaven
  Shall fill his mouth with mould.

I do not know when that was written. But I can make a guess—or at any rate I can ask a question. How often after 1895 has Housman's voice quite that decisive clear ring? In 1895 that bright ring of words was with him; and in the years lying near to that golden year he could command it occasionally. It was not with him, I think, in 1922. In that year he went through what he had written, meaning to give the world the last poems that it should have from him. He took from his notebooks the best that he could find; or so at least he supposed. It was better to print it while he lived than have it misprinted and mispunctuated after his death. The task of ordering it affected him strangely. Sorting his old sins, he got going again. He did what he had not done for more than a quarter of a century; he wrote on end something like a dozen new pieces. The first of them (the date given is, in fact, 1921) shows what was happening. It is not so much new writing as rewriting:

He stood, and heard the steeple
  Sprinkle the quarters on the morning town.
One, two, three, four, to market-place and people
  It tossed them down.

Strapped, noosed, nighing his hour,
  He stood and counted them and cursed his luck;
And then the clock collected in the tower
  Its strength, and struck.

Having written that, he might well feel self-assured. Picking it up, whether in the deserts of Sahara or in Trinity Great Court, who would not have cried 'Housman'? It is the authentic miracle. But was it worth it? He was sixty-one. Yet not one jot of advance can you ascertain, whether in technique or idea, upon the Housman of thirty-five. It is the old talent, but alas! the old napkin.

For one or two of the 1922 pieces I confessed, when they appeared—not knowing the dates—a liking beyond what I had for a good many of the poems of *A Shropshire Lad*. If they were less good than what had gone before, they had more of softness and tenderness. An example is furnished by the lines beginning 'In valleys green and still . . . '. But in general these 1922 poems are neither the old miracle nor anything new. In truth the miracle is that, crowding them into *Last Poems*, Housman crowded out for the sake of them a world of far better youthful stuff, saved to us now by the tact and judgement of Laurence Housman.

'Youthful stuff' is perhaps not the right term to apply to the poetry of a poet five-and-thirty years old. And we are brought back here to Housman's real tragedy. Until he was thirty-five he wrote 'very little'. During five months of a single year, 1895, out of the bitterness of his heart, or the pit of his stomach, he was a poet. For the rest of his life he was engaged in what a poet at least might be forgiven for thinking the most useless of conceivable human occupations, the textual criticism of Latin texts. That is not exact biography; for in 1914 he wrote his 'Mercenary Army' lines; and one or two of his best pieces fall, verifiably, outside what I have called his *annus mirabilis*; of others the dating is only conjectural. But it remains substantially true that as a practising poet he begins and ends in the early part of 1895. I know nothing quite like it in literary history. In truth, it does not make sense. What is worse, it does not make mystery. Nor did Housman want it to make mystery. All his utterances on the subject of his own poetry run in the other direction. It is a perfectly simple matter, he would have you know: he was not in the habit of writing poetry; when he did so it was, so far as he could judge, because he was not feeling very well. Nor, when he talks like that, is it just casual talk, private, among friends. His one great public performance, the Cambridge lecture on *The Name and Nature of Poetry*, says it all again, in effect. Indeed, it says more; for it says, if not in so many words, yet sufficiently in the sum of its implications, that nobody in his senses writes poetry except because he is feeling not very well. In the eighteenth century all the world felt horribly well. Nobody in his senses wrote any poetry at all. What poets had happy and healthy England? 'These four: Collins, Christopher Smart, Cowper, and Blake. And what characteristics had these four in common? They were mad.' Poor Gray! As Matthew Arnold says, he 'never spoke out'. He wrote his *Elegy* in a country churchyard, and not in the county asylum. He had the misfortune not to be as mad as a hatter, and he must give place to Smart. It is odd, let me say in passing, that it is in Blake, of all our poets, that Housman finds the idea of a poet most fully actualized. In Blake, 'the meaning is a poor foolish disappointing thing in comparison with the verses'; and it is just on that account that he is, for Housman, a better poet than Gray. Some of

Housman's melodies are, perhaps, studied on Blake. But of essential likeness to Blake he has surely nothing. His poetry bristles with plain meanings. Brutally meaningful, it challenges all his critical utterances. When he gave his lecture he had been twenty-two years in Cambridge. During that period he had written perhaps a dozen poems. 'I have improved', he said, 'in some respects and deteriorated in others; but I have not so much improved as to become a literary critic, nor so much deteriorated as to fancy that I have become one.' He concludes his lecture characteristically: 'Let me retire from my incursion into the foreign territory of literary criticism . . . I will not say with Coleridge that I recentre my immortal mind in the deep sabbath of self-content; but I shall go back with relief and thankfulness to my proper job.'

By his proper job he means the criticism of Latin texts, and of persons other than himself who had the infernal impudence to edit them. Not for him, truly, 'the deep sabbath of self-content'. After London, he found Cambridge an asylum; 'in all senses of the word', he added ungratefully. But he was not such a lunatic as to write poetry there. He kept by him the old notebooks, stuffed with the old verses. He kept also, we now know,[1] another notebook, filled with unkind things which he meant to say about this or that person, whenever he got the chance. Think of it!—those famous critical incivilities and inhumanities, all reach-me-down! Someone applied to him, not long since, in my hearing a contemptuous phrase; it was a young man, and as such I forgave him, but he spoke of Housman as 'a

[1] *A.E.H.*, p. 77.

cantankerous old introvert'. That is to take things on the wrong plane and, in being modern, to forget how dark a region the soul of man is, how mysterious an abysm the pit of the stomach.

Rereading Housman's lecture, I am freshly reminded how rare a thing is good criticism. 'Once in a century', he says, 'or once in two centuries, the literary critic does appear.' But it does not much matter; if he came, like the washing, once a week, the purpose which he serves is (in Housman's account of it) not specially useful. For he does not bring critical truths; but only 'personal opinions'. If he says that 'things are thus and thus', it does not follow that they are so, but that he thinks so—at least, that he says he thinks so. If he says that Collins and Cowper, Smart and Blake, are the only poets of the eighteenth century, it is his personal opinion, and you may take it or leave it. Why I should take it, unless it happens to be true, I am left to guess. But this is all very old; it was venerable claptrap when I was in my cradle. Yet a good many people like it; and one thing about it I like myself—the delightful liberty which it promises. Take in any century the four poets you like best; call them the best poets of their times; and no man shall say you nay. I have the fancy to play Housman at his own game. But a century is more than I can manage, and I will hold to the last ninety years—the period between the death of Wordsworth and the year 1939. That in that period, or in any other, the most certifiable poetry is that of the certifiable lunatic, not even Housman could persuade me; though if a man were looking for lunatics the last twenty years would be a paradise for him. But leaving the lunatics, who, for the ninety years I name, are our four best poets? About the first of them I have never had any doubt; nor can I doubt but that here I have Housman with me. Housman put first the poet who, of all our poets, is perhaps the least like Blake. It could never be said, I think, of Matthew Arnold's poetry that 'the meaning is a poor foolish disappointing thing in comparison with the verses'. Housman thought him, even so, a great poet. He thought him a great critic into the bargain; though he can hardly have admired his critical opinions—if they have any truth, his own have none. What he thought of Stevenson must be guessed from the degree in which he is like him. I should like to have heard him on Rupert Brooke—they must have been dons together at Cambridge. Brooke's poetry also stands obliged to Stevenson for a good deal in its style and manner. Matthew Arnold, Stevenson, Brooke, Housman—I do not say that these are, since Wordsworth died, our four best poets; and if I did, nobody would believe me, unless it were Housman. But there would be something in it, beyond the expression of favouritism. With Matthew Arnold died the grand manner in poetry. Stevenson—though to remember him as a poet at all makes a man sixty, and over—Stevenson leads in the modern manner. With this lost leader are Brooke and Housman. The march of the modern manner becomes, thereafter, confused; till it is a question whether it would not be better, instead of going on, to go back.

OLIVER GOLDSMITH

THE quality of Goldsmith's fame is attested by its successful resistance to two classes of mischief: the calculated impertinence of the prigs—such men, that is, as Boswell and Macaulay; and the miscalculated kindness of the sentimentalists—chief among them Thackeray. The prigs, perhaps, do not greatly matter; here, as everywhere, their art is self-defeating. The sentimentalists are a more serious trouble, since it is no part of virtue to show hardness towards natures which have none of it nor could sustain it. Yet a humane criticism may so far, perhaps, assert itself against Thackeray, and the tribe of rhapsodists, as to recall that Goldsmith is primarily important as a *writer*. In the profession of a writer he achieved success after failing in almost every other profession known to man—medicine, law, the Church, keeping school, keeping shop, play-acting, flute-playing, begging. Of his adventures in these many callings the record is uncertain; and he himself attached no exaggerated value to them as sources of experience giving reality to his writing. He had begged, or fluted, his way across Europe; but it had taught him that 'we see more of the world by travel, and more of human nature by remaining at home'.[1] The crosses of his early years he took, it is likely, more in his proper character—the character, that is, of the 'good-natured man'—than the popular accounts of him would have us to believe.

[1] *Present State of Polite Learning*, ch. xii.

The reactions of this character upon political and literary circumstances are at least as interesting as the vicissitudes of Goldsmith's personal fortune. He was born in 1728. A new king had just confirmed Walpole in that long lease of political power to which Goldsmith liked to trace the decline of English letters. He died in 1774. The same year witnessed the accession of Louis XVI to the throne of France, and the year following the beginning of the American War of Independence. These synchronisms have their significance for the study of a poet who touches greatness in two poems expressly composed to convey the truths of political economy. That the greatness of *The Traveller* and *The Deserted Village* is not given by their economics is easily said. Yet *The Traveller* at least is not properly placed if these are forgotten. It was begun just before this country became involved with France in the Seven Years War; and it was finished in the months following Wilkes's attack on the king in No. 45 of the *North Briton.* The latter portion of it might be described as the reflections of a Good-Natured Man overtaken by the first mutter of the storm of Human Freedom. The piece owes something to Addison's *Letter from Italy*. Both poets had begged their way across Europe; but that the ornate beggary of a pension from Lord Halifax had taught Addison anything, or had rendered him either acute or just in his observation, nothing in his poem indicates. He came back with what he took out: his pension, and the comfortable Whiggish conviction that Great Britain was the natural and exclusive home of Freedom and Good Government. Only so far as this conviction has truth or nature is there anything of either in his poem.

Goldsmith brought home the poverty in which he started out; but the kingdoms of the world and their want of glory had persuaded him that government, good or bad, contributes little or nothing to man's happiness. Those parts of life, or of the heart, which 'kings or laws' can materially affect are few. The grandeur of the human soul consists in its good nature; and those states are best governed of which the citizens are sufficiently good-natured to put up with what they are given.

The Traveller, especially the concluding portion, should be read side by side with a poem which consciously imitates parts of it—the *Descriptive Sketches* of Wordsworth. When the reader has made the comparison, he should make another equally instructive. He should read Goldsmith's essay 'On the Distresses of a Common Soldier' (*Essays*, xxiv), with its companion piece, 'On the Distresses of the Poor' (*Citizen of the World*, cxix); and these two pieces he should compare with the delineation of the same distresses furnished by Wordsworth's *Female Vagrant*. The strength of Goldsmith is his humour, of Wordsworth his want of it. Both made the mistake of supposing that the rest of the world were like themselves. The more serious mistake was that of Goldsmith; for if there is a real distinction between good and bad, it is probably nowhere so obvious as in the case of 'kings and laws'. Men are serious in demanding justice, and it is silly to tell them not to mind. Souls gifted with that humorous stoicism which makes Goldsmith, as a man and as a writer, so attractive are comparatively rare; and humourless souls with red revolution in them at least a good deal commoner than Goldsmith believed. In one particular

Goldsmith erred grievously: it did not occur to him that men who are good-natured enough to forgo their own rights can be fanatical in their assertion of the rights of others.

Accordingly in *The Traveller*, and in a less degree in *The Deserted Village*, the reader must be as easy-going as Goldsmith himself not to be sensible of a certain intellectual incompetence. Social and economic conditions were moving in the direction of a change greater than any since the break-up of the Middle Ages; and to the self-imposed study of these altering conditions Goldsmith brought inaccurate observation and trivial comment—the same faults, in fact, as made him, in the circle of Dr. Johnson, a disputant almost contemptible. In the exercise, on the other hand, of the arts of feeling and memory (each of which has its proper genius) he abounds in grace and truth: virtues which communicate themselves even to his diction. His was not a crusading nature; but he waged a humorous and effective war against the dominant fear of the 'low' in incident, sentiment, and speech. 'It were to be wished', he writes,[1] 'that we no longer found pleasure with the inflated style that has for some years been looked upon as fine writing, and which every young writer is now obliged to adopt if he chooses to be read. We should now dispense with loaded epithet and dressing up trifles with dignity. . . . Let us, instead of writing finely, try to write naturally.' That in verse Goldsmith is always as good as his principles, that *The Traveller* and *The Deserted Village* are everywhere free from conventional diction, it would be rash to affirm. But

[1] *Present State of Polite Learning*, ch. x.

they have at least a purer and truer diction than the rest of the poetry of their day. Of his prose style, the praise may be set a good deal higher. Goldsmith was a born writer, writing upon any subject well and easily. Boswell, it is true, has alleged that he consciously imitated Johnson; but the two styles are, in fact, essentially opposed: and what Goldsmith says of 'dressing up trifles with dignity' hits Johnson hard. In the qualities required for the profession of a *general writer*, Johnson was not well endowed; Goldsmith has all of them in perfection. 'Goldsmith', says Johnson himself, with splendid justice, 'was a man who, whatever he wrote, did it better than any other man could do.' He essayed nothing, perhaps, which required the highest powers; but in the kind of writing which he undertook he had an easy adequacy, a style in perfect adjustment with temperament.

His plays are certainly not a negligible part of his achievement. He has himself analysed for us the faults of the fashionable comedy of the time. 'The Comic Muse long sick', was 'a-dying'. She was dying of her own 'gentility', of her fussy fear of the 'low', of her addiction to 'sentimentals'. These were, in a great degree, infections of literature as a whole; and it is the grand merit of all Goldsmith's writings (a merit best illustrated, perhaps, by the *Vicar of Wakefield*) to be clean of all of them. To dispel them from contemporary comedy, however, was a business requiring a high quality of faith. Goldsmith speaks of himself as coming to comedy 'strongly prepossessed in favour of the poets of the last age'. His most valuable prepossession was, in fact, one which he shares with all considerable dramatists.

It is probable that he had picked up in his *Wanderjahre* some first-hand acquaintance with stage practice; but his greatest asset was his masculine conviction that what the theatre wishes is in tragedy to be made to cry, and in comedy to be made to laugh. 'On my conscience', he writes, 'I believe we have all forgotten to laugh in these days.' Outside Goldsmith and Sheridan the eighteenth century can show no comedy at which a man could conceivably laugh. It was not done; and it was not easy to persuade people that it should be done. *The Good-Natured Man* is not among the best English comedies; but it at least gave Goldsmith the chance of developing a character which he understood thoroughly, and it furnished his public with a reasonable excuse for permitting themselves to be amused. 'Uncommonly low', said the *London Chronicle* the next morning. But Goldsmith had made his public laugh; and before they had time to relapse into gentility and 'sentimentals', he gave them, in *She Stoops to Conquer*, one of the masterpieces of the English stage. The plot involves a ludicrous experience of his youth, when he upon one occasion mistook the house of a gentleman in Ardagh for an inn. Nothing is so good for the world as that now and again someone should break in on its gentilities, command its best cheer, and rouse it to something of catholic inn-keeping quality.

Let us not forget, however, that Goldsmith belongs after all not to the inn (any more than to the city or the club), but to the fields. There his treasure and his heart is. He had laid up his treasure in the long years of his vagabondage; and his most characteristic effects, those effects in which he illustrates most movingly our common nature, proceed from the pieties of youthful memory. His true spiritual riches are the poverty of his youth; and his best skill, to illuminate tenderly for each of us the deserted village of the heart, its broken roads, and unfinished purposes.

POETRY AND THE CRITICAL ART

Best of the delights of literature is, I think, after reading poetry, reading about it. Philosophy and History are, perhaps, graver departments than Criticism, serving deeper interests. But they less serve delight; and when they do—as with Herodotus and Plato—we may still ask whether that is a happy chance or something that properly belongs to their character. What makes Criticism especially delightful is, I feel, not merely its naturalness—to talk about books is even more natural than to write them—but its freedom. The critic, I mean, unlike the philosopher and the historian, has not got to break his heart about truth. His primary concern is, not the true, but the interesting.

So at least I like to conceive Criticism; and some such conception of the critical office I have it at heart to commend to you; at a time when, as it seems to me, we no longer look sufficiently naturally either at poetry or at the criticism of it. Such a conception seems, I know, to a good many persons to depreciate the critical art somewhat unfairly. Yet as soon as we try to conceive it differently, either we drive it upon science—so that it is no longer an art—or we fail to distinguish the criticism of poetry from poetry itself. That the critic of poetry must be a poet has been said so often that the only excuse for not believing it is the history of Criticism itself; from which, if there is anything to be learned, it is that the best critics have been, not poets, but poetically minded men—or poets up to a point, the Dryden point, say, or the Sainte-Beuve point. That the criticism of poetry is a science is less often said than implied. Yet it has been said, by good critics; and it seems to be implied in the currency of many of our critical phrases: as when we speak of 'the evolution of poetry' or 'the laws of poetry'. There is no doubt an evolution of poetry. But it *is* a poetical one: that has, before anything else, to be remembered, and to remember it is to forgo science. That there are laws of poetry I should be sorry not to believe. But, like the laws of nature, they have always seemed to me very well able to look after themselves—and, indeed, to have done so with rather more credit than the laws of nature. From Homer to our own day it is astonishing how steady they have kept. In contrast, from Thales to Einstein how incorrigibly unstable have not the laws of nature shown themselves! Who of us, even now, feels any confidence in them? There are, of course, periods in the history of poetry when accredited opinions are brought rudely into question, when the practice of poets is seen to vacillate and tradition to go into the melting-pot. We are living, perhaps, in such a period now. Yet I do not know that, at the present time, there is a greater uncertainty about our poetics than about our ethics. Morals are as much in the melting-pot as everything else—or so it seems. But is anybody, in fact, really much frightened about it? We take it all perhaps a little uncomfortably, and a little as though it served us right. In a way, it does. The laws of morality are, in the main, so well ascertained that we have become, if I may use the expression, a degree cocksure about them. It is good for us to be shaken up a little. Till the other day, similarly, we were a degree cocksure about the laws of poetry—or about some parts of them. The present shake-up was needed. But I am not disposed to take too heavily the confusions of the time. They are not, I feel, sufficient to obliterate the substantial difference which there is between good and bad in poetry or right and wrong in ethics. When I am told that there is no such thing as good and bad in poetry, but only what we like and dislike, I comfort myself with the reflection that on the whole we mostly like, all of us, the same things, and that it is improbable that we do so by accident. Those agitations of opinion which periodically trouble our theory and practice rarely live so long as we apprehend or make the large alteration which they threaten. The truth is that poetry, founded in the heart of man, answering to spiritual needs in him, is only a little less unchanging than human nature itself.

It is this that gives to the critic of poetry—if only he will take it—that security and freedom which is so especially delightful and so much a condition of art. I say 'if only he will take it'; because about the criticism of poetry, as about poetry itself, we have become, I fancy, in recent years sophistical. We are for ever making difficulties—in criticism where there are none, and in poetry where there are only mysteries. We tend too much to drag the critic into the region of ultimate things, as though he must open his mouth in metaphysic or not at all; and as though to open his mouth in kindness, to adorn common truths with variety of illustration, to speak from character and experience, counted for nothing at all. It troubles me that we seem not able to look at criticism more naturally, and somewhat more after the manner of the older critics. I cannot but think that the best critics—after whose example it seems proper that we should fashion our definition of Criticism—have been those who have vexed themselves least with ultimate questions, and written from a certain security of heart. Of the best critics the primary aim has been always, I should suppose, to make, about one kind of literature, another. Of Dryden, one of the very best of critics, someone has said that, when he writes upon Shakespeare, he maintains the directness and simplicity of 'one mortal man and good writer talking happily about another'. No praise could be more proper for Dryden, nor any better description perhaps be offered of the office of the critic generally. Dryden has to be reckoned, it is true, among those who have supposed that the best critics of poetry are the poets. 'Poets themselves', he writes, in the preface to *All for Love* (that play of his in which he is most a poet), 'are the most proper, though I conclude not the only critics.' Even so, he is not wholly consistent with himself; he forgets his best-remembered epigram, he forgets that he has elsewhere told us that 'the corruption of a poet is the generation of a critic'. I fancy, indeed, that the poet in whom he seeks his critic had better have been called, more simply, a poetically minded man. We want, not a poet, not an immortal man, but a 'mortal man and good writer'. And we want him 'talking happily', and humanly, in 'the other harmony of prose'. We ask of him, neither aesthetic nor rhapsody, nor laws out of Sinai, but good and happy writing.

If Dryden asks that his ideal critic should be a poet, he does so, I suspect, because he knows himself to be a good critic and supposes himself to be a better poet than he is. If today we wish, some of us, to commit the criticism of poetry to the poets, that proceeds, I fancy, from a certain scepticism in us. We no longer believe that there is anything to be said about poetry—the only comment upon it is some other poetry. That such a view studies—as it purports to do—the honour of poetry, I find it difficult to believe; to entertain it is, I feel, not to think highly of poetry, but really not to believe in it at all. If the best poets are not always the best—and are sometimes the worst—critics, that is not because they do not believe in poetry, but because they do not believe in anything else. They do not believe, for example, in prose, nor in knowledge, nor in common experience—in any experience which does not end in itself. But this, which in the poets is faith in poetry, is in us only scepticism—it is not to believe in poetry. If poetry ends in itself, there can be no criticism of poetry. And of course, if all poetry were equally good, and if it were always apprehended by poets, if there were only perfect poetry, and we were all the perfect audience of it, there *would* be no criticism. But if we are less than poets, it is not to believe in poetry when we set our faces against criticism. That the criticism of poetry is not itself poetry means only that we are men, most of us, and not gods. That it is not the supreme harmony is no reason why we should not essay to make of it 'another harmony'. A mortal man and good writer talking happily about poetry in the other harmony of prose—what is Man that, when he succeeds in being to that degree interesting, we should despise Criticism?

To write or talk about poetry should be, of all literary behaviours, the most obvious and natural. That we should leave it to the poets is not natural. Not how poetry affects the poets—which is all that the poets can tell us (nor can they tell us that *critically*)—but how it affects ordinary men: just that is the mystery of poetry, just that the business of criticism. Nor is it natural, or proper, to leave it to the aestheticians; for it is not nearly so hard for a camel to go through the eye of a needle as for an aesthetician to be also a man of letters. Nor, again, are the laws of poetry like the laws of zoology, that we should leave poetic criticism to the scientific historian. And once more, the laws of poetry are not a penal code, that we should commit the administration of them to the reviewer. 'There is always justice enough left in mankind', says Dryden, 'to protect good writers.' But not enough perception, it may be, to discover them. It may be true, as Dr. Johnson alleges, that 'no genius was ever blasted by the breath of criticks'. Yet unless Criticism is, in fact, valueless, unless any man's judgement in poetry is as good as another's (which nobody believes), great poetry and great poets do stand in need of the critic.

The poet, the aesthetician, the scientific historian, the reviewer—have I excluded all these from the field of Criticism only to introduce, in the room of them, the dilettante? It can only seem so because I have not yet said what should not need saying—first, that before a man can criticize poetry he must care for it intensely, and secondly, that a critic must know what he is talking about. The first point I need perhaps not labour, save to add that to an intense care for poetry there must go some quality of character, some depth of spirituality. But that Criticism must be founded on knowledge is perhaps less obvious than it seems. Here again, however, I deprecate making difficulties where there are none. What the critic of poetry must know is plain. Primarily he must know poets and poetry, and he must know good from bad. Of course, no knowledge is easy, but this is not more difficult than other kinds: it requires different aptitudes from those necessary to knowledge in other departments; but given these aptitudes, it is not more difficult. That we only get to know by knowing already is a mystery common to all knowledge, and not peculiar to poetical knowing.

Such a critic as I have in mind, then, is not a dilettante, because, to criticize poetry, he must both know something and be somebody. One of the Latin writers, I think Cato, defined the Orator as *vir bonus dicendi peritus*, 'a good man acquainted with speaking'; meaning, I suppose, to emphasize the necessity of character as an ingredient in eloquence. If I were to define my ideal critic as 'a good man acquainted with poetry', I should offend, I know, all those good men acquainted with poetry who exist to see that poetry takes no infection from moral ideas. If poetry has nothing to do with moral ideas, still less has the criticism of it. Even so, I have always had an uneasy feeling that Dr. Johnson, had he been a less virtuous man, would almost certainly have been a less good critic of poetry. Nor am I sure that one-half of the merits of Hazlitt in criticism do not in fact proceed from a consuming zeal which he has for freedom and righteousness. In the sense in which Dr. Johnson had virtue, it would be hard, I suppose, to call Hazlitt a virtuous man. Yet this consuming zeal for freedom and righteousness Hazlitt has; and it makes a world of difference to his criticism. Perhaps, however, I shall be safer if, instead of asking that my critic be a good man, I content myself with the phrase that I have already used, and let 'mortal man' suffice. With that phrase, I mean that I want my critic, first, to be in some sort a critic of life. If knowledge of the world can make him that, well and good; if not, he will need spiritual perception. But secondly, I want him to be, as I have hinted, not too ultimate. Nor yet too Olympian —and with the Olympians I class not merely the metaphysicians, but prigs and pedants, and men too good to be true, or too true to be persuasive, and, generally, stiff men wanting human quality. I ask a sufficiency of nature.

I ask a sufficiency of nature. But I do so because I believe the criticism of poetry to be an art. That it is not an easy art follows from the very definition of it—it can never be easy to write prose about poetry.

The final judgement of poetry, let me say in conclusion, rests not with the critic, but with a far simpler person; a simpler person, but having powerful allies. 'By the common sense', says Johnson, speaking of Gray's *Elegy*, 'By the common sense of readers uncorrupted with literary prejudices, after all the refinements of subtlety and the dogmatism of learning, must be finally decided all claim to poetical honours.' 'About all things on which the publick thinks long,' he says elsewhere, 'it commonly thinks right.' To this court must come both the loftiest poetry and the latest verse—to the uncorrupted sentiment of the ordinary reader, sitting in judgement with Time.

ERASMUS IN PRAISE OF ENGLAND

A DUTCHMAN by birth, by temper and habit a European, Erasmus has, none the less, very special claims upon the regard of Englishmen. He spent six years of his life in this country; and if fortune had been kinder, he had hoped, he tells us, to end his days here. Some of his best and truest friends were Englishmen—More, Fisher, Colet, Warham—the best and truest Englishmen of their time. Perhaps, indeed, this was the only country in which he never had an enemy—the rather absurd quarrel with Lee belongs to Louvain. Some of his most important work was done in England. In England he wrote the *Praise of Folly*; and in England was conceived and executed the greater part of his greatest undertaking, his edition of the Greek Testament. In England he did most of his work upon Jerome.

In the last months of his life England was a good deal in his thoughts. The last work which he saw through the press was his *Preacher*. The preface to it is occupied with memories of Fisher and More and Mountjoy. A long passage in the first book is devoted to the praise of Warham. One of the last letters which he wrote is addressed to Warham's successor, Cranmer. Whether Cranmer ever received the letter we have no means of knowing: the autograph draft of it is preserved, unpublished, in Copenhagen.

> Daily [Erasmus writes] my health grows worse and yet worse; so that I am compelled to refrain, not only from the old hard work, but from any kind of study, and am almost wholly confined to my bed. I suffer grievous pain. . . . But this is the Lord's doing, who uses knife and cautery, that he may be merciful in the life everlasting.

Another unpublished letter of the same date is preserved in the British Museum, addressed to yet another famous Englishman, Thomas Cromwell. The purpose of both letters is the same—to thank the person addressed for a gift of money. Neither Cranmer nor Cromwell, Erasmus confides to a friend, would have sent him money if they had read what he had written in his *Preacher* about Fisher and More and Mountjoy. Mountjoy had been chamberlain to Queen Katherine. One of the last letters which Erasmus received is from Chapuys, the Imperial ambassador at the court of Henry VIII. In it Chapuys speaks of the comfort which Erasmus's essay *On Preparing for Death* had brought to the dying Katherine—'that immortal pattern and perfection of womanly goodness'. By a curious irony, the book which brought so much comfort to Queen Katherine was dedicated to the father of Anne Boleyn. So strangely was Erasmus served by his habit of being unable to take sides. The only book which he dedicated to Katherine she received coldly. Yet it handled a theme which could hardly have been indifferent either to herself or to Henry—the *Institution of Christian Matrimony*. One of four books dedicated to Henry was the Paraphrase of the third Gospel. The Paraphrase of the fourth was translated into English by Henry's daughter, Mary. She was helped by Nicholas Udall, who, with other scholars, was responsible for a complete English version of all Erasmus's New Testament Paraphrases. The patroness of the undertaking was Henry's last—and luckiest—queen, Katherine Parr; and the book had a distinguished fortune later, since Injunctions of both Edward VI and Elizabeth placed it in every church in England.

In general, however, Henry and Henry's family served Erasmus disappointingly. But he took all his English disappointments good-temperedly; and his praise of England and Englishmen is nearly everywhere generous. For English learning he had a genuine admiration, the expression of which is sometimes, no doubt, interested. Having listened in Oxford to Colet and Linacre and Grocyn, it is hardly worth his while, he says, in 1499, to go on to Italy, except for sight-seeing. In 1519, again, a well-known letter to Mountjoy extols both Oxford and Cambridge. In both those years he was seeking preferment in England. But in 1528, when he wrote his *Ciceronianus*, he praises English scholarship—Oxford scholarship in particular—generously and, at so late a date, disinterestedly. In the same year, in his treatise *On Pronunciation*, the true use of royal and ecclesiastical wealth is illustrated from the example of the English universities. How well he knew Oxford it is difficult to say. He calls Corpus (founded in the year in which his Greek Testament appeared) 'one of the principal glories of Britain'. After that, it is disappointing to find that at least twice he confuses it with Christ Church. That he taught at Cambridge the Greek which he learned in Oxford is prettily said, by Gibbon, but false. Erasmus learned his Greek in Paris. He did, however, learn in

Oxford, from Colet, that without Greek he could do none of the things he had set his heart on. His Greek Testament belongs, not to Oxford, but to Cambridge. It is true that, when published, it was banned there. But apart from his praises of Fisher, there are passages in his writings which indicate that he did not regard sweetness and light as an Oxford copyright. In his Apology to Sutor, he recalls that Archbishop Melton, 'a man of weighty learning, blameless life and engaging disposition', required a knowledge of the classical literatures from candidates for holy orders—the students of Cambridge, he says, bear witness how well he exhorted them to the humanities. In the *Reason of True Theology*, again, he notes with satisfaction that in Cambridge purely verbal disputes occupy a less place than they did, with the consequence that philosophic studies 'flourish not less, but more truly'.

He is probably the only foreigner who has ever praised the English climate. For the poem in which he praises it he, no doubt, hoped to be paid. But as the same praises recur in his letters, we must suppose him to be serious—but a foreigner. Our habit of never opening windows he thought detestable; and equally detestable our habit of spitting on the floor. Our custom of kissing upon every possible pretext he could not sufficiently praise. It was not enough, he tells us, to welcome the coming guest with kisses and to speed with kisses the parting guest. The guest who went out for a walk was kissed; the guest who came in from a walk came in for kisses; and, indeed, he was hardly allowed to cross the room without being kissed. Most of this kissing seems to have been done by 'nymphs'—so he calls them—'of divine countenance, soft and yielding, very much better nymphs than the Muses'. All this was easily and pleasantly learnt. Learning our language was a less easy business; and perhaps the only compliment which Erasmus never paid us was to learn English. He had a pupil in Cambridge called Smith. Smith's father complained that the boy learned nothing because his tutor could only talk Latin. At least, the boy learned Latin, Erasmus rejoins. He remembers this boy, perhaps, in the essay *On Pronunciation*, where he tells us that the English tease foreigners by asking them to say 'Smith'—the final *th* of which no foreigner could master. Warham gave him a living in Kent, but dispensed him from the duties of it because of his ignorance of English. Yet if he never preached sermons in English, he listened to them; for in his essay on preaching, 'the delivery of English preachers', he says, 'is like the barking of dogs, rather than like human speech'. This he attributes to the fact that 'the language is mostly made up of monosyllables'. It is said, he remarks in the same essay, that the English language, like some other modern tongues, is capable of literary effects not inferior to those of Latin. 'England', he says elsewhere, 'has men who have done for her what Dante and Petrarch did for Italy.' Allen supposes him to be thinking of Gower and Chaucer. Chaucer and Wyatt are perhaps more probable—they are mentioned together in the *De Poetis* of Lilius Gyraldus, a younger contemporary of Erasmus. If Erasmus does not name them, it is because they are only names to him. Nor can importance be attached to his often-quoted praises of Skelton—except as tutor to Prince Henry, Skelton meant nothing to him.

Of the many compliments paid by Erasmus to this country perhaps the most surprising is to be found in an epigram which he wrote at Cambridge in the autumn of 1513, having for its subject the Battle of the Spurs. Did you come out to battle, he asks the French, only for the purpose of running away? Was this a contest in strength of arm, or in swiftness of foot? The verses are strangely out of character—in general, in the wars of Christian kings Erasmus sides with neither combatant. His essay on war in the *Adages*, often translated, has been used in modern times as a pacifist pamphlet. So too his *Complaint of Peace*. One of Erasmus's dearest friends was at the seat of war in 1513: the tone of Erasmus's letters to him is flippant.

Only one of Erasmus's books was printed in England—a Latin translation of Plutarch *On Keeping in Health*. It was printed 'not altogether unattractively' in London, probably by Pynson; but no copy of it survives. The *Praise of Folly* was printed in Paris; the Greek Testament in Basle. But both books belong, in a real sense, to England. The *Praise of Folly* arose out of his friendship with More. Colet's influence drew him to edit the Greek Testament. These two books were determining, implicating, and so far fatal that they gave to his life a direction in many ways false and unfortunate. They carried him whither he would not; withdrawing him from the pleasant places of humanism, stationing him, timid and unreliable, on the battlefield of the Reformation. His heart was in 'good letters'—i.e. the Christian writers read humanely, the classical writers read Christianly. He had no heart to strive and cry. But these two books placed him in a situation where striving and crying was a condition of life. If Erasmus sounded the first trumpet of the Reformation, it was in a kind of bookish innocence. Afterwards he was never quite able to credit what he had done.

> What I am trying to do [he writes in the *Spongia*] is to advance the study of good letters and, so far as lies in my power, to make theology purer and simpler. To this aim I shall adhere my life long. The disposition of Luther, whether friendly or hostile, will affect me not at all. I judge him human and liable to err. Luther and the Lutherans shall pass away, but Christ abideth for ever.

His Greek Testament, like everything else that he did, was done in a hurry. He was anxious, it is said, to anticipate the edition of Cardinal Ximenes; which, though it did not appear until 1522, was already printed. As a critical undertaking his Greek text is plainly inferior to that of Ximenes. It was accompanied by a Latin version which was certainly intended in some sort to supersede the Vulgate. Erasmus afterwards, it is true, disclaimed this intention. But he laboured heavily to prove that the Vulgate was not the work of Jerome; a contention refuted, not only by modern scholarship, but already in his own time, and decisively, by Eugubinus. As a translator he is sometimes perverse. When the angel Gabriel salutes Mary as 'gratia plena', Mary, he insists, is 'greatly troubled' because, as the Greek shows, the words are capable of an amatory significance. In 'Repent ye, for the Kingdom of Heaven is at hand', he replaces Jerome's 'poenitentiam agite' ('do penance') by 'resipiscite' ('get a new mind'): a change which deeply affected Luther's thinking. But this happy stroke conducts him to the unhappy, and absurd, contention that the word 'penitence' is connected, not with *poena*, punishment, but with *pone tenere*, which he interprets as 'to reflect afterwards'.

A first-rate Greek scholar he never was: he was plainly capable at times of bad Latin scholarship. None the less, his Greek Testament is one of the great landmarks of European learning. It is so, and will remain so for all time, not from the exactness of its scholarship but for the reason that, with whatever faults, it vindicates for scholarship nobly and decisively the spirit of free inquiry. It has a further importance, which is accidental. Owing to the use made of it by Aldus and Stephanus it became, in effect, the received text of the New Testament; a position from which it was not finally dislodged until near the close of the nineteenth century. The Jerome, published in the same year, was part of the same effort. Erasmus wished, first, that students should have the Scriptures in the language in which they had been written; and secondly, that they should interpret them in a human and real fashion. The second of these two objects could only be attained by going behind the schoolmen, back to the Fathers. Herein lies the importance of the Jerome, and in a less degree of Erasmus's other editions of the Fathers—Cyprian, Hilary, Ambrose, Augustine, the Latin Irenaeus, the Latin Chrysostom. He began with Jerome, because with Jerome he felt special sympathy. He preferred Jerome's Latin to that of Cicero—with happy consequences to his own; and to Jerome may be traced much in the temper and method of his criticism.

These works do not belong with the great monuments of critical scholarship. The same is true—indeed, much more true—of his editions of some of the great classical writers. Yet in all these departments he did important work. The importance of it consists partly in the fact that it was done in *all* of them—in the range of his interests, in their catholic and liberal accent, he beats the exact scholars. As a preface-writer, an introducer, a summarizer of essentials, he is unsurpassed. If there is a journalism of scholarship, he is its greatest practitioner. Even in his New Testament may be found many of the better elements of journalism.

The *Praise of Folly* Erasmus spoke of always as a piece of foolishness. He had wished to amuse the world with it; and he succeeded in amusing the Pope, a worldly man. But he had not wished to fire a crusade. The book, says Froude, 'flew over Western Christendom. . . . Like an explosion of spiritual dynamite, it left monks and clergy in wreck and confusion. . . . It was delicate and witty, running through the heart like a polished rapier and killing dead in the politest manner in the world.' There is something here both of mixed metaphor and of exaggeration. Instead of speaking of 'spiritual dynamite' it would be simpler, perhaps (though it would not sound so well), to call the *Folly* a theological squib. It is a squib which today dances and crackles a little disappointingly. Both in history and in the history of literature the book has its proper place, and will continue to be read. Yet, when we wish to say of it, what a fine piece of literature this is! common honesty plucks us back, and, what a fine piece of journalism, we say, this *was*!

What fine journalism, again, do not the *Colloquies*

enshrine, especially the more friendly of them; what delightfully drawn pictures of places, people, social life and manners! 'The best and brightest', Froude has properly said, 'are the pictures of England.' Is it to praise Charles Reade, or to disparage him, when we say that the best of what we owe to him in *The Cloister and the Hearth* is coextensive with what he himself owes to the *Colloquies*? The touch of the *Colloquies* is more modern than that of the *Folly*. With not much disguise, many sections of them might parade unchallenged with the best effects of *Tatler* and *Spectator*, *Elia* and *Table Talk*.

Of the Lives of Erasmus the best is still that of Froude; Erasmian in its brightness and lightness, in its careless learning and eager prejudice. But more than forty years have gone by since Froude drew his finely sympathetic picture—he attempted, in any case, no more than a sketch. A new Life was projected by Allen, a pupil of Froude, but so far unlike his master that he seemed constitutionally incapable of either prejudice or inaccuracy. Allen might well have been expected to give us the perfect biography. In one particular, indeed, he might have proved faulty—he was not worldly enough. So much of Erasmus bears a mixed accent, the dialect of the dove obscurely variegated by notes borrowed from the subtlest of all the beasts of the field. Too often Allen's innocency of ear heard it *all dove*.

But if Allen did not know the world, no one in the world knew Erasmus as he did. The Life which he did not live to write must be written, when someone else writes it, out of his edition of the Letters. As a document of the history of the times the Letters have primary importance. Yet they are to be valued, ultimately, not as they enable us to place Erasmus in history but as they help us to disengage him from it, to redeem him out of history into literature, placing him where, in truth, he longed to be. Not the *Folly*, nor the *Colloquies*, but the Letters, are his best piece of literature. What he did in scholarship, whether biblical, patristic, or classical, has been superseded—though not the fine free temper of it. That fine free temper shines also in the Letters, being indeed one of the elements of literature. Here and there the student may be interested to explore other parts of Erasmus's writings. The addict of devotional literature —a rare character perhaps today—may read with profit the *Christian Soldier's Manual.* No one, again, who has a taste for good Latin invective should miss the *Spongia.* It is that work of Erasmus which does least credit to his heart—Hutten, whom he assails, was dead. Yet nothing that he wrote illustrates so well his tremendous effectiveness as a writer for occasions. Nowhere is his Latin more lively, his mood more deadly. But from these and like excursions our curiosity will be glad to get back to the Letters. In the immortality of their readableness Erasmus lives securely, immune from the discredits of circumstance.

Allen edited a Selection from the Letters. Erasmus was always interested in devising books from which schoolboys might learn Latin pleasantly; and here, neglected by schoolmasters, is just such a book. With its admirable easy Latin, its delightful pictures of Englishmen and English life, its touch with living interests, it might, without dispossessing Caesar and Livy, supplement them usefully. It would serve to admonish students of the continuity of Latin learning; and to remind us all of the very real services of Erasmus to education. His life was in good letters; and he wished to win the world to good letters. But he had, perhaps, in connexion with them, no dearer concern than to humanize the theory and practice of teaching. The education of boys, as he knew it, was inhumane, and in many particulars inhuman. The subject is one to which his writings make frequent reference—his interest in it was perhaps intensified by his intercourse with Colet. Wherever he speaks of schoolchildren and the teaching of them, what he says has humility and tenderness.

This faithful servant of good letters has summarized his achievement, as he himself saw it, in some sentences of a letter to Cardinal Gattinara:

> It will not be gainsaid that it was I who gave new life to the study of the tongues, and of good letters. When theology in our universities had degenerated into sophistic chatter, it was I who recalled it to the fountain-head, to Scripture and the older and juster commentators upon Scripture. I strove to re-awaken to goodness of life a world which had fallen asleep amid empty forms and ceremonies. I gave myself to no party. I gathered no party about me.

Of that summary, Time, older and wiser by four centuries, has not essentially qualified any of the particulars.

SIR HENRY SAVILE: 1549–1949

OXFORD colleges do not much affect, I think, centenary celebrations—we too much take our great men for granted. Merton, in this matter, is surely no better than the other colleges. In 1914, it is true, we celebrated the septemcentenary of the birth of Roger Bacon. That he was born in 1214 is very uncertain; and it is quite certain that he never belonged to this college. But that did not matter. Here in this Hall all the learned world lunched, blessing Bacon. Among the guests, I recall, was the librarian of the Vatican, Achille Ratti, later Pope Pius XI. He made a speech which would have been better appreciated if it had not been in Latin, and if he had used some other pronunciation than the Roman.[1] But he made up for it after lunch. After lunch, happily and harmlessly, in a nearby college, he played 'Up Jenkins'—for which the Italian is, we discovered, 'Avante Ienkin'. Has ever a Pope of Rome, before or since, played this forgotten game? In 1932, another luncheon in this same Hall commemorated the tercentenary of a less great man

[1] That he should use this pronunciation was natural. But, as Pope, he was specially interested, later, to enforce its use in the churches of all countries (see his letter to Cardinal Dubois, 30 Nov. 1928, *Revue du chant grégorien*, 33, 69): 'romanam latinae linguae pronunciationem probamus . . . optamus vehementer ut omnes cuiusvis nationis episcopi . . . eam . . . sequi velint.'

than Bacon, but a more authentic Mertonian—Anthony Wood. The principal speaker was Lord Grey of Fallodon. Round the memory of one of the most unamiable of men, Grey's amiable personality played ineffectively.

In 1945 we let pass unnoticed the quatercentenary of the birth of Sir Thomas Bodley. For that we were not to blame—the war was still with us. The ghost of Bodley, I think, if we are kinder today to Savile than to himself, counts it some grace in us. Sir Henry Savile, courtier, scholar, mathematician, founder of the Oxford professorships of Astronomy and Geometry, for four years a scholar of Brasenose, for thirty-seven years Warden of Merton, and for five-and-twenty years Provost of Eton, a friend of Bodley and of the Bodleian, was born on 30 November 1549. Of the grandeur of his services to learning Anthony Wood says—perhaps a little too grandly—that they were such as 'will make his memory honourable not only among the learned but the righteous for ever, till the general conflagration shall consume all books and learning'. At any rate, the quatercentenary of his birth deserves not to go by without salute. Whether it would have been better noticed by a luncheon than by a lecture I am not prepared to say. But the lecture, let me say, is no fault of mine; save in so far as it is an old failing in me to do as I am told.

To the unlearned Savile is best known, I should suppose, by two sayings which have passed for witticisms, but which were, I think, meant ever so seriously. The one of them is preserved in Bacon's *Apophthegms*. 'Mr. Savill', says Bacon, 'was asked by my lord of Essex his opinion touching poets; who answered my lord: "He thought them the best of writers, next to those that write prose".' Savile was not being clever. He did not like clever men; and he hated genius. This appears more plainly in the second of the two sayings which I have mentioned. The preservation of it we owe to Aubrey. Savile, Aubrey writes, 'could not abide *witts*: when a young scholar was recommended to him for a good witt, "Out upon him" (Savile cried), "I'le have nothing to doe with him; give me the plodding student. If I could look for witts I would goe to Newgate, there be the witts".' Among the Merton wits of Savile's time were Cuffe (who was hanged) and a relation of his own, a good poet, but a dissolute man, Thomas Carew. I do not easily forgive him, even so. Really, I believe, he liked dull men. For anyone, that is a bad temper; it is a particularly bad temper in the head of a college.

Savile passes for one of the great heads of colleges. Elected Warden of Merton in 1586, he was, in effect, the nominee of Queen Elizabeth. The queen, says Aubrey, 'favoured him much'. For besides being 'a learned gentleman, as most was of his time', he was 'an extraordinarily handsome and beautiful man; no lady had a finer complexion'. In the Gheeraerts portrait of him in Bodley—of which this Hall shows a tolerable copy—he does not look quite all that. But for the Virgin Queen he had appeal. The instructions which she sent, touching his election, are interesting and characteristic. She wished the fellows of Merton to choose their own Warden freely, in accordance with their Statutes. But they would, she trusted, 'seeke to concur with her Majesty's inclinations'.

In the histories of Merton, Savile figures as indisputably

the greatest of wardens; his only possible rival being that grand enemy of the humanities, Bishop Fitzjames. Savile did a good deal for the humanities. But in one particular he was a little like Fitzjames. Fitzjames was a shameless pluralist, holding the office of warden in conjunction with three successive bishoprics. Savile was Warden of Merton for thirty-seven years, during the last twenty-five of which he was Provost of Eton. The Merton Register furnishes a very full account of his reign; and the casual reader—indeed, the attentive reader—would suppose that never a complaint was raised against him. He appears everywhere as the perfect warden. Only recently has it become possible to read between the lines of the register. Not eighteen months ago the college acquired a series of letters which throw a new light, I think, on the character of Savile. They belonged at one time to the miscellaneous Selden-Hale collection, of which the greater part has now, I believe, found a home in the Library of St. Paul's Cathedral. The letters must be thought a degree damaging to Savile. Hitherto he has passed for one of the few wardens with whom the fellows never quarrelled. But the perfect peace which breathes from the college register is a fake—it is plain, indeed, from the letters, that the register has been, in some parts of it, deliberately falsified. The letters show the fellows quarrelling with the warden about a great many things. Instead of the perfect warden of tradition, they reveal a warden thought by many of his colleagues, by the seniors among them especially, to be very imperfect indeed.

Some hint of the truth may be found already in Aubrey. 'He was not only a severe governor', Aubrey writes, 'but old Mr. Yates (who was fellow in his time) would make lamentable complaints of him to his dyeing day, that he did oppress the fellows grievously, and he was so great and a favourite with the Queen, that there was no dealing with him.' 'Old Mr. Yates' lived to tell tales till he was well over ninety. But, outside Aubrey, not much notice has been taken of him. In the newly found letters we encounter him as a young man, lending support to the older fellows in the war which they waged against Savile.

The war began—or our first records of it begin—in 1598. From that year date the earliest of the new letters. Some details, however, they furnish from the years immediately preceding. The causes of the war are, in part, obscure. But the immediate occasion of it seems to have been the unwillingness of the senior fellows to continue to accept as sub-warden a favourite of Savile's, Thomas Master. Master was one of the five senior fellows. In a good many matters of moment, in particular in the election of college officers, the government of the college lay with the warden and the five senior fellows. Already in Savile's second year as warden, Master had been elected sub-warden. Elections to this office were made annually. It is notable that from 1587 to 1602 (the year in which he ceased to be a fellow) Master held the office of sub-warden almost continuously. But he was better liked, it would seem, by the warden than by the fellows. The warden's sub-warden, the complaisant deputy of an absentee—so we may plausibly conceive him. In 1597 he took a living. His acceptance of it was taken by the fellows as an excuse for not reappointing him as sub-warden—only once before had they failed to re-elect him. The living was supposed to be a *uberius beneficium*, disqualifying the holder of it from holding with it a fellowship. But ejected from the office of sub-warden, Master was not prepared to give up his fellowship. Like the warden, he believed in pluralism. An appeal was made to the Visitor. The Visitor decided in favour of Master. The seniors, in a letter which might well be considered insolent in its terms, appealed to the Visitor to reconsider his decision, and not to perpetuate 'a fret and ulcer', as they phrased it, in their society. The letter is signed by all the seniors (Master excepted) and by six junior fellows, among them young Mr. Yates. But the Archbishop of Canterbury stood firm.

A month later, on 1 August—the date set apart by custom for the election of college officers—the senior fellows took their revenge. The warden had notified the fellows that 'by reason of sicknesse' he could not appear on 1 August; and the elections must wait his coming. But the seniors had had enough of Savile's absences—and of the presence of Master. If Savile must be for ever absent, he should have a deputy whom he did not bargain for. They proceeded, contrary to his express instructions, to elect officers. As sub-warden they re-elected Jasper Colmer—for whom they had displaced Master in the year preceding.

Neither of the election made nor of the meeting at which it was made does the college register preserve any record. But the minutes of the meeting in fact survive among the newly acquired letters. The votes given by each of the fellows are recorded. At the foot of the minute paper Savile has written a note in his own hand: 'And I, Henry Savile, Warden, dissenting from the nomination made by the above, do by the authority given to me by the Founder pronounce this election void, and remit the whole matter to the judgement of the most Reverend the Visitor.'[1]

And now the letters spring a surprise upon us. In this war of dons the queen intervenes. One of the new letters is a letter from the treasurer of her Chamber, Sir John Stanhope (later Lord Stanhope of Harrington). At the instance of the queen, Stanhope writes to the Visitor, Archbishop Whitgift, conveying to him the queen's wish that he shall proceed at once to 'an exemplary punishment' of the fellows who were vexing her favourite. The letter is couched in terms so strong as to leave the archbishop no choice but to comply with the queen's pleasure. Strong as the language which he uses is, Stanhope fears that he may have been 'to sparynge in delivering her Majesty's pleasure', and adds a postscript urging 'expedition'. Expedition the Visitor used. Immediately on receipt of Stanhope's letter, he drafted a letter to the fellows of Merton pronouncing their 'disordered proceedings' to be 'utterlie voide', and appointing Master as sub-warden. The offending seniors are ordered to appear before him at Lambeth in the first week of Michaelmas Term. The letter is a much corrected draft, in Whitgift's autograph. Of a fair copy of it there is no trace either in Merton or at Lambeth.

Thirteen in all of the new-found letters deal with this incident—six of them are in the autograph of Savile. Of none of them is there so much as a hint either in the

[1] Et ego Hen. Savile custos a nominatione per predictos facta dissentiens, auctoritate mihi a fundatore concessa electionem hanc irritam esse pronuntio, arbitrioque reverendiss(imi) patroni eam totam reservo. Hen. Savile custos.

Merton Register or in Whitgift's Register. In Whitgift's Register, however, there is extant a letter of Whitgift to the warden and fellows of Merton, pronouncing judgement. The letter is dated 1 October 1598. That the terms of it are nowhere entered in the Merton Register can hardly be accident. Colmer, the irregularly elected sub-warden, is deprived of his fellowship. Of three other senior fellows the fellowships are suspended. From one of them, Fisher, we have a letter of penitence, written to the archbishop, craving remission of sentence. On behalf of another, Brizenden, there is a letter to the archbishop from the Mayor and Corporation of the City of Oxford. Brizenden is spoken of as 'the publicke and onlie preacher to our citizens', and as a man not capable of deliberate wrong-doing.

Within five days of the receipt of the archbishop's letter Colmer fell ill and died. We know this only from a rather brutal reference in a letter of one of Savile's friends, John Chamberlain. 'The Warden of Merton Colledge', Chamberlain writes (to Sir Dudley Carleton), 'hath got a great victorie of his fellowes and raunsommed and punished divers of them and amongst the rest expelled Master Colmer who of griefe or curst hart died within five days after.'[1]

I cannot but think it an ugly story. The silence of the register upon all these happenings is not a little remarkable. It can hardly be accident that it suppresses altogether two important rescripts of the Visitor; hardly accident that it has no record at all of a college meeting of which our letters preserve the draft minutes; hardly accident that, listing

[1] *Letters of John Chamberlain*, ed. N. E. McClure, 1939, i, p. 52.

the officers for the year 1598, it lists, as though they had been appointed in the ordinary way, officers appointed *extra morem* by the Visitor to replace those elected by the fellows.

From 1598 to 1602 Master, the *fons et origo* of all these troubles, continued to hold without a break the office of sub-warden. The victory of Savile might well have been thought complete. The Merton records continue to breathe peace. That it was a false peace, and that Savile's victory was less entire than it might seem, appears from two other letters of the recent find. Neither of them carries any date. But both may be assigned, I think, with some confidence, to the years 1601–2. The first of them bears no signature, nor is the person to whom it is directed anywhere named. Addressed vaguely as 'Your lordship' and 'Your honour', he is to be identified, I feel pretty certain, with the Chancellor of the University of Oxford, Thomas Sackville, later Earl of Dorset. The letter speaks of him as acting in conjunction with the Archbishop of Canterbury. Sackville belonged to the class Savile hated—he was a poet. The letter sets out in detail the numerous grievances of the fellows of Merton against their warden. Pluralism, absenteeism, favouritism, corrupt administration of the properties of the college—these are the principal counts in the indictment. The letter catalogues at length 'the inconveniences of one man's beinge Mr of more houses of learninge than one at once and together'. They are specially great when the two houses concerned are Merton and Eton. Even if these inconveniences did not exist, the Statutes of Merton, the letter argues, make it quite plain that 'the heade of this college havinge gotten the headship of the other ought not to be esteemed heade of the former'.

What action was taken upon this letter we have no means of knowing. But the second of the two letters I have mentioned is a letter of Savile himself, addressed to the archbishop. It consists of five folio pages, closely written, in Savile's best hand—never a good one, but with this letter he has taken trouble. The Chancellor of the University, it appears, had approached Savile directly and urgently upon two subjects; upon both of which he hoped shortly to join with the archbishop 'in a motion to her Majesty'. The one was the absence from college of some of the heads of colleges, the other the presence there of their wives. It was plain to Savile that the Chancellor was in fact inviting him to resign his office in Merton. The next thing that will happen, he says, is that the Chancellor of Cambridge will tell him to give up Eton. Is he not, he asks, as much an absentee from Eton as from Merton? His letter is, throughout, cynical and worldly. It is quite likely, he allows, that he could be replaced by a better man. But some stronger reason than that should be found for depriving him. If the founder of Merton did not like pluralists, he should have drawn his statutes more plainly. He proceeds to defend his position by the precedent of Fitzjames and some other pluralists. As for wives living in college—there, he thinks, the chancellor may find support in the spirit, if not in the letter, of the statutes. So much does he feel this that he is perfectly prepared, he writes, to put his wife out of college, asking only that other heads of colleges should do the like. What he says here of his wife should be read, perhaps, in the light of an anecdote preserved by Wood. Lady Savile, Wood says, was bored sometimes by Savile's excessive preoccupation with Chrysostom. 'Sir Henry,' she said, 'I would I were a book too, and then you would a little more respect me.' Some third person, unnamed, joined in. 'Madam,' said he, 'you should be an Almanack that he might change every year.' This jest, we are told, Lady Savile did not much like; we may suspect in her, as in Savile, a deficiency of humour. Incidentally, she preferred, it would seem, Savile the mathematician to Savile the scholar. I say that recalling some verses addressed to her by a Brasenose don.

> If it is the business [he writes (and he seems to think that it is)] of the wife to rule, and the husband to obey, it was under your direction that mathematics were set going in Oxford. But even if the wife's business consists merely in letting her husband have his own way, you deserve as much praise as he does.

That I find donnish—the don gone gallant. What seems certain is that Savile preferred his books to his wife.

Whitgift's answer to Savile's letter, if ever he made one, is not extant. But whatever answer he got, Savile, I feel certain, had the archbishop with him—and the queen. At any rate he retained, for another twenty years, in conjunction with the Provostship of Eton, the office of Warden of Merton. If he owed these offices, in the first instance, to the favour of Elizabeth, his security in them he owed, it seems clear, to the favour of James I. In 1604 he entertained the king at Eton, and was knighted. His best deeds, in any case, belong to James's reign.

The first of his published works had been printed at Oxford in 1591—a translation of the *Histories* (Books I–IV) and *Agricola* of Tacitus, dedicated to the queen. The dedicatory letter is interesting. Not only did the queen, we are told, hold Tacitus 'in great account', but she had written 'admirable compositions of her owne' (presumably historical), and had made 'rare and excellent translations of Histories', translations which (says Savile) 'infinitely exceeded the originals'. Savile's primary purpose, he insists, in printing his Tacitus was to induce the queen to publish something of her own in the same kind. Whether anything is known from other sources of Elizabeth's exercises in history, I have no idea. Whatever they were, I feel sure they were not dull. That Savile's translations of Tacitus either 'exceed the originals', or come passably near them, I am not able to persuade myself. Far rather, here, I feel, is a dull man translating a writer never dull—without knowing it, he has fallen in with what he most hated, a wit. He hopes, he tells the queen, that 'the pleasing taste to the palate' of Tacitus' Latin has not been wholly lost in his translation. But it has—the praises of Ben Jonson notwithstanding.

Savile, says Aubrey, citing Hobbes, 'would faine have been thought to have been as great a scholar as Joseph Scaliger'. That greatness he certainly has not. In the history of scholarship, none the less, he has, if only by his edition of Chrysostom, an assured place. The book furnishes the first example in England of critical scholarship on the grand scale. In the first quarter of the sixteenth century, four successive editions of Chrysostom in Latin had excited curiosity about the original from which they derived. Must this golden-mouthed Greek continue to be golden-mouthed only in Latin? The project of a Greek Chrysostom had engaged the attention of eminent scholars: isolated texts of Chrysostom had been edited in the Greek by Erasmus and John Matthew Giberti. It was left to Savile to give to the world the first complete Greek Chrysostom. The book was never a best-seller; partly because it was pillaged by the two Morelli for their Paris edition of 1609–33. The Prince Palatine accepted a presentation copy, sending Savile, in return, two silver-gilt cups and a ewer, worth together, we are told, some £50. For a copy presented to the United Provinces Savile got a gold chain of about the same value. The Signory of Venice, for a copy received through Sir Dudley Carleton, sent a gift, unspecified, of yet greater value. The eight volumes presented to the Signory may still be seen, sumptuously bound, in the Library of St. Mark's at Venice. But 'he makes no great riddance of his volumes', Chamberlain writes, in 1614, 'and I feare they will lie on his hand, or on theyrs to whom he shold leave them'.[1] The original manuscript of his book Savile presented to the library of his own college. Of the printed edition that library still has two copies. But of the manuscript there is no trace. Scholars were disappointed with the book. Yet it was a century before it was superseded by the more complete and scholarly edition of Montfaucon.

[1] *Letters*, i, pp. 434, 436, 510.

Another piece of work which engaged Savile's talents as a Greek scholar was the Authorized Version of the Gospels and Acts. Of his part in this undertaking we would wish to know more. That it was a leading part may be inferred from the fact that the committee of translators did much of their work in his Lodgings in Merton. Books necessary to them were transferred from the college library to the Lodgings. So much the college register notes, giving the names of the scholars who worked with Savile—the list of names agrees with other extant lists, except that there is no mention of Ravis, the Dean of Christ Church. (It would be interesting to know what were the books which the Merton library supplied. Of books lent, somewhat earlier, to some of the translators, the writer of the register had in mind to give a full list. They used, he says, 'the following books'. But he was tired, or idle; and his list is not there.)

If Aubrey speaks slightingly of Savile's scholarship, he is generous to him as a mathematician. The thirteen lectures on Geometry which Savile gave from his own Chair of Geometry in 1620—they were published in the year following—perhaps no man living has read. But at least they mark an epoch in English education. At the time when they were delivered, there was—Savile himself tells us—no geometry in England at all. The first lecture is entirely occupied with telling the audience who Euclid was. In the last lecture, Savile, old and ill, takes a rather pathetic farewell of Oxford. 'Weary with years', he says, '*cyclos artemque repono*. Among my successors in this Chair there will be, likely enough, men more vigorous in body and of more lively mind.' Oxford will come nearer so to 'the innermost mysteries of geometry'. What these are we are not told. But he commends to the special attention of students the *fifth* book of Euclid. It sounds a little trivial. Yet what Aubrey hints may well be true; and what Savile did in and for mathematical studies should perhaps be accounted his most enduring monument. It was not nothing that he brought from Cambridge to Merton, as the first occupants of his two chairs of mathematics, two mathematicians of distinction in Henry Briggs, inventor of the Briggsian logarithms, and John Bainbridge, who had just acquired a perhaps cheap fame by his observations on the comet of 1618. It is not often, I fancy, that professors of mathematics turn poets. But the death of Savile drew verses from both Bainbridge and Briggs. That they were not offering mere perfunctory compliment I infer from the fact that Bainbridge wrote no less than four poems for the occasion; three of them in Latin—in the fourth he rises to Greek. Savile, Bainbridge says, was, while he lived, a god among men: in particular he was a god to the astronomers. He has passed now to the skies. Bainbridge promises his students that, hereafter, when they survey together the starry heavens, he will show them the star of Savile new-risen. Briggs keeps nearer to earth. He is concerned to emphasize Savile's real accomplishment in mathematics—the professorships which he founded were in subjects which he knew well and taught well.

Not content with founding and endowing two professorships of mathematics, Savile founded and endowed, for the use of his professors, a mathematical library—in 1884 it was incorporated with the Bodleian. He deserves to be remembered very specially as a lover of libraries. For the library of his own college, at all times, he did much. For the year 1556 there is extant a complete catalogue of the manuscripts and printed books in that library. The printed books number not much above 300. During the first ten years, alone, of Savile's reign there were added to these 300 hardly less than 1,000. Much of this increase must be attributed to the energy of Savile himself. When he lay dying, the Merton Register records that fellows of the college were brought to Eton to select from his library such books as they cared to have for the library of Merton. His brother, Thomas Savile, and the unfortunate Cuffe were both employed, in their travels on the Continent, buying books for Merton. It was Savile, I feel sure, who was responsible for bringing to Merton the library of the Cambridge jurist Betts. Manuscript catalogues survive—one of them annotated by Savile—which reveal the Merton library, at this time, as a great law library. Some of Betts's books passed from Merton to the Bodleian—a gift from the college to Sir Thomas Bodley. They may still be seen on the Bodleian shelves, in their distinctive binding, Betts's initials stamped large on the cover. From his own library Savile gave to the Bodleian not only printed books but manuscripts. Nor did his interest in the Bodleian end there. In 1609 Merton—which meant Savile—gave to Bodley (on a promise to pay at some later date) the timber, or a part of the timber, used in the building of the Bodleian. It was Savile, yet again, who brought to Oxford two of the master-craftsmen employed by Bodley to build his library

—their names deserve record: Acroyd of Halifax, the *faber lapidarius*, and his associate Holt, the *faber lignarius*. They had just completed, when they began on the Bodleian, the Great Quadrangle of Merton.

To Savile's friendship with Bodley more than one writer bears testimony. I have noted a substantial testimony to it in the Merton bursarial accounts for 1598. In the spring of that year Bodley visited his old college. The occasion was marked by a dinner; for which the meats cost 57*s*. 4*d*, the wines 11*s*. 6*d*. The pound has suffered, since, devaluation; and the dinner was, I have no doubt, better than our dinners are today. Bodley and Savile were friends. But they had not always been friends. From the Merton Register and Archbishop Parker's Register in Lambeth it is possible to reconstruct an episode in the early academic life of these two great men which shows them, not only not friends, but belonging to sharply opposed factions. Bodley became a fellow of Merton in 1563, Savile in 1565. For the academic year 1566–7 Bodley was dean of the college, or rather, one of three deans—a single dean did not suffice, I suppose, in those days, for law and order. The deans of this year were not much liked; two of them in particular, Bodley and a certain Ralph Latham, were very much *dis*liked. 'Grave charges', we are told, were brought against them—which means, perhaps, no more than that there was a good deal of carping. But the college became divided into two parties; the party of law and order and strict Protestantism, Bodley's party, and a rebel faction of which one of the adherents was Savile. There were provocative actions on both sides—with the details of which I need not bother you. At one point the Visitor, Archbishop Parker, intervened. The warden was absent—he was Warden Mann, employed by the queen as her ambassador in Spain. The Spanish ambassador in London was one Guzman. 'They sent me a Goose-man', said Elizabeth. 'I have sent them a Mann-goose.' The warden was absent; and the rebel faction had no use for the Visitor. Ten of them, of whom Savile was one, went so far as to address to him a very improper letter. The letter, signed by all the rebels, Savile included, may still be seen in Archbishop Parker's Register. It challenges, in terms flatly contumacious, not only a decision of the Visitor, but his whole *ius patronatus*. 'A dangerous and bold attempt', Strype, the archbishop's biographer, calls it; and speaks of the authors of it as 'young hotblades'. Savile was a youth of eighteen. I should not have expected, even so, to find him among the hotblades. I should like him the better for it were it not that, thirty years afterwards, he showed himself so great a hater of hotblades, so insistent that Archbishop Whitgift should exercise against them the full powers of his *patronatus*—to the hotblades of 1567–8 Archbishop Parker had shown himself ludicrously indulgent.

In this ancient college the two great names are still Savile and Bodley. Five years after Savile's death, 'What one college', wrote George Hakewell, 'ever yeelded . . . two such . . . Heroicall Spirits?' With that praise, from the head of another college, we may be content. This quatercentenary set me working upon documents about Savile which I could not properly neglect. If here and there I have seemed a little out of love with him, I am sorry. That I came to bury Savile, not to praise him, I would not have you suppose. Some of the documents I think a little damaging —to a greatness, even so, real and rememberable. In that rememberable greatness this college, Brasenose, and the university, stand today complacent partners.

MAX AND MERTON COLLEGE

SOME weeks ago I met an American in the Merton Garden. I knew that he was an American, because the garden is private. But 'I am full of curiosity', he told me, 'about this college'. Two of his curiosities he thought I could satisfy. 'Am I right', he said, 'in thinking that this is the oldest college in the world? and wasn't it here that Max Beerbohm received his education?' I told him that the college was perhaps not quite as old as that. But that it was Max's college. How much of his education he got here, I was not sure. 'Are there any memories of him here?' he asked me. 'His name is known here,' I said, 'and perhaps nowhere else in the world. To us he is Henry Maximilian Beerbohm. But to the rest of the world just Max. What happened to the Henry, why he dropped it, why *Who's Who* knows nothing about it, I have no idea.' '*Who's Who* doesn't know what's what', said my friend. 'There's a lost romance, I vow, with that lost Henry. Very few Americans', he added, 'are called Henry, except Longfellow. And Longfellow's a different class to Max. Can you tell me where he lived? Somewhere within these old walls he had rooms?' 'Max lived in Mob,' I said, 'in what used to be called Bachelors' Quad.' This meant nothing to him, but he wrote it down eagerly. I took him to Max's old rooms—they are now a part of the library—'the oldest library in Great Britain' I was careful to explain.

Since Max's day they have been a good deal changed, internally. They are now a reading-room—in Max's undergraduate youth nobody read. In one particular they are less medieval than they were when Max knew them—they are full of carvings by Wren, the remains of the chancel-screen which Wren made for the college chapel. Wren's screen was taken from the chapel (and relegated to a lumber-room) by Butterfield the architect. On another monstrous behaviour of Butterfield's Max's eyes used to rest daily. The windows of his room looked on the Butterfield building in the Merton Grove. In a paper of Oxford reminiscences printed, I think, in the periodical *Oxford*, Max speaks of the pain with which he always contemplated this Butterfield atrocity. But he calls it red-brick. Ugly as it is, it is, in fact, perfectly good Bath stone. For Max, I must suppose, Butterfield was red-brick everywhere because of Keble. Another distinguished occupant of Max's rooms was, at an earlier date, Lord Randolph Churchill. 'I think it would please Mr. Churchill', said my American friend, 'to know that his father lived in rooms destined to be occupied by Max.'

From Max's rooms we went to the Senior Common Room. There Max is happily remembered in bronze and in pencil. The bronze is a charming statuette by Kathleen Scott (Lady Kennet), showing Max in 1907. On one of the walls is a drawing of Max by William Rothenstein, made in 1928. In the same room, hidden away, are a few rough caricatures by Max, showing some of the Merton dons of his time—Brodrick, who was warden, Bowman, who succeeded him in that office, and George Scott

('Black Scott'), who was, I fancy, Max's tutor. I doubt if Max liked either Bowman or his tutor. With the other dons he is likely to have had little contact. Some of them were distinguished; four of them were outstanding philosophers —F. H. Bradley, William Wallace, John Burnet, Harold Joachim. But Max never had much metaphysic. English literature was represented, inadequately, by Napier. In the year in which Max became an undergraduate, Andrew Lang was made an honorary fellow of the college. Max was made an honorary fellow in 1945. In 1936 the college dramatic society acted *Savonarola Brown* in the college hall. Max took a friendly interest in the performance, and drew a picture for the cover of the programme.

All these things I explained to my American. 'Well, there do seem', he said in parting, 'to be some memories of Max in Merton still.' There are; and they are all kindly.

PHALARIS AND PHALARISM

SIXTEEN HUNDRED AND EIGHTY-NINE was one of the busy years. William III became King of England, Stillingfleet Bishop of Worcester, Aldrich Dean of Christ Church—three excellent appointments. Bentley went to Wadham as tutor to the young Stillingfleet, Swift to Moor Park as 'servant' to Sir William Temple. In June of this year Swift—whom Macaulay calls 'a disagreeable young Irishman', but who was, in fact, like Bentley, a disagreeable young Yorkshireman—wrote an agreeable but uninspired Ode to the Hon. Sir William Temple. The ode was 'in the manner of Cowley'—both Sir William and his lady had the good taste to admire Cowley, and Swift had the good sense to appear to do so. He had been looking through some of Temple's essays—essays in which, while he is a little like Cowley, he misses Cowley's happiest merit, that of knowing when to stop. That he had read the essay *Upon the Gardens of Epicurus* his ode everywhere intimates. But he had not neglected an essay destined to greater celebrity:

> They purchase knowledge at th' expense
> Of common breeding, common sense,
> And grow at once scholars and fools;
> Affect ill-manner'd pedantry,
> Rudeness, ill-nature, incivility,
> And sick with dregs of knowledge grown,
> Which greedily they swallow down,
> Still cast it up, and nauseate company.

The lines are suggested by the paragraphs on pedantry which conclude Temple's essay *Of the Ancient and Modern Learning*. Temple's paragraphs were to furnish the hint, nine years later, for the character of the Pedant in 'Boyle against Bentley'.

When he wrote the essay *Of the Ancient and Modern Learning*, Temple was a little past sixty. It is hard if a man may not take advantage of that eminence of years to make essays of his likes and dislikes. And Temple begins so gently and naturally ('Whoever converses much among the Old Books, will be something hard to please among the New . . .'); and concludes so sweetly and tenderly ('I shall Conclude with a saying of Alphonsus (surnamed the Wise) King of Aragon; That among so many things as are by Men possessed or pursued in the Course of their Lives, all the rest are but Bawbles, Besides Old Wood to Burn, Old Wine to Drink, Old Friends to Converse with, and Old Books to Read . . .'); and throughout writes so much from temperament, that cavil and contradiction seem inapposite. The mixture of vanity is, as Hume says, 'rather, a recommendation'. Temple genuinely preferred horticulture to statesmanship, literature to science; and in his essays he sought no more than to express the character of one governed by these genteel prejudices. He had his favourite authors, as a man of sixty—or perhaps, any gentleman—is entitled to have, without giving his reasons. Among them was King Solomon; and in *Some Thoughts upon reviewing the essay upon the Ancient and Modern Learning* (published posthumously) he closes the discussion with a sentence from Ecclesiastes: 'The Thing that has been, is that which shall be, and there is no new Thing under the Sun.' In 1689 the tragedy of his son's death weighed heavily upon him; and the Preacher's doctrine of the vanity of human things was very present. 'Strange and vain the earthly turmoil'; and not a little unreal the new knowledge. 'Old Books to Read' still meant something; the modern world with its Gresham College and its well-advertised scientific discoveries very little.

For Temple 'modern learning' means the learning of the Royal Society; and it is surprising how small a part of his essay—eight short paragraphs, less than two pages of the 1740 folio—is occupied with literature. Fontenelle's *Digression* and Perrault's four dialogues had been almost exclusively concerned with the comparison between ancient and modern art and literature; though the *title* of Perrault's book seems to promise a discussion of the sciences. But the issue on which the 'battle of the books' was joined in this country was not a literary issue. That ancient literature, considered merely as literature, is better than modern was a thesis which nobody in England was the least disposed to contest. Temple was welcome to prefer Virgil to Boileau, Homer to *Gondibert*. What could not be borne was his disparagement of modern science, his contempt for 'the studies, the writings, the productions of Gresham College'. It was past bearing that, in the age of Newton and Halley—when the *Principia* had been already two years before the public—he should write that 'there is nothing new in astronomy to vye with the Ancients, unless it be the Copernican System'. It was past bearing, again, that he should pooh-pooh Harvey—whose great discovery was given to the world in the year in which Temple was born.

The quarrel was between literature and science. Wotton, who prepared the answer to Temple, was not a man of letters. He was a clergyman interested (like Bentley) in bringing to religion the support of science. He had taken his degree at Cambridge in 1679, an infant prodigy of twelve. In the summer of that year he had been on exhibit at the Royal Society, chatting with Burnet and Lloyd, who 'did not believe there had the like appeared in the world'.[1] Burnet and Lloyd were very likely right. As a child of five Wotton was a competent scholar in Latin, Greek, and Hebrew. To these tongues he had added, when Burnet and Lloyd met him, Arabic, Syriac, and 'most of the modern languages'.[2] In divinity, law, 'all the sciences', history, chronology, mathematics, he was 'universally and solidly learned'. Boys of twelve were not eligible for membership of the Royal Society. But so soon as he reached the age of twenty-one, Wotton became a fellow.[3]

Temple's book had been published in 1690. Wotton's *Reflections upon Ancient and Modern Learning* was not ready until the summer of 1694. Why Wotton, or the Royal Society, waited so long it is not easy to say. 'All or most of the materials' for the book, it is said, were supplied to Wotton from 'other hands'—Halley and the surgeon Charles Bernard were particularly mentioned. Bentley and

[1] Evelyn, *Diary*, 6 July 1679.

[2] In 1722 he preached a sermon in Welsh (Nichols, *Literary Anecdotes*, iv, p. 262).

[3] Birch, *History of the Royal Society*, iv, p. 557. Bentley had to wait till 1694, though he matriculated at Cambridge in the same year as Wotton.

Evelyn were implicated. A dozen years previously Evelyn had himself written a 'discourse' in which he

> did attempt to shew how far a gentleman might become very knowing, and to good purpose, by the onely assistance of the modern languages. . . . Nor was it without purpose of one day publishing it; not for ostentation, but because 'twas written with the virtuous design of provoking the court *fopps*, and for incouragement of illustrious persons who have leasure and inclynations to cultivate their minds.

But he had mislaid his essay. He was in close touch, however, with Wotton, while Wotton was writing the *Reflections*. Wotton's delays are perhaps to be explained out of his character. If he spent four years writing the *Reflections*, he spent the rest of his life writing nothing, or nothing worth reading. Hearne speaks of him, in 1711, as 'a very debauched man', and mentioning his death in 1727 makes grave charges against him. A more friendly notice of him records that owing to 'difficulties in his private fortune' he quitted his living in 1714; and attributes to 'the eccentricity of his conduct' the fact that advancement in the Church was consistently withheld from him. In 1694—or for that matter in 1679—he seemed marked down for the highest preferment. 'But some dark shadow came'; and the most learned man in England died poor and despised.

In the year in which Temple's essay was published, there had matriculated at Christ Church two clever Westminster boys, the Hon. Charles Boyle and his friend Anthony Alsop. Boyle, destined to be fourth Earl of Orrery, was a grand-nephew of Robert Boyle. Assigned as pupil to Atterbury, he received both from his tutor and from the dean those attentions which his title and talents deserved; in return, Aldrich and Atterbury supped familiarly at Park Place. Two pretty compliments the dean paid his favourite. He wrote for his use a handbook of logic, *Artis Logicae Compendium*, which, first printed in 1691, still held its place in the Oxford schools in the middle of the nineteenth century—readers of Clough's *Bothie* will remember the Oxford tutor ('the grave man, nicknamed Adam') who, albeit 'shady in Latin', was 'topping in Plays and Aldrich'. The other compliment was more embarrassing. Temple had remarked that 'the oldest Books we have are still in their kind the best' ('a thing observ'd even by the ancients', Bentley comments, drily). But 'the two most ancient that I know of in prose', he had added, unluckily, '. . . are Aesop's Fables and Phalaris's Epistles'. Everyone knows how Lord Baldwin embarrassed the booksellers by praising Mary Webb. Similarly, when Temple praised Phalaris and Aesop, the demand for these authors was beyond what the booksellers could meet. Aldrich, 'finding Mr. Boyle was a good Grecian, desired him to put out a new Edition of the Epistles of Phalaris', an author 'likely to inspire a young Man of Quality with Sentiments agreeable to his Birth and Fortune'. Alsop was commissioned at the same time to prepare a text of Aesop.

Alsop was the better scholar of the two. But it is hard, as Byron said, if a young nobleman may not 'have his merits handsomely allowed'; and Boyle had industry and cleverness beyond the common. His letters to Atterbury exhibit him as a serious—perhaps slightly priggish—student, genuinely interested in literature. Already in 1691 he had been reading Temple's essays. At the end of that year, and in 1692, he was engaged in making a translation of Plutarch's Life of Lysander—it was, no doubt, this piece of work which caused the dean to think him a 'good Grecian'. Nor was he a bad Latinist. In 1693, in conjunction with two of his Christ Church friends, he composed a Latin poem—a bucolic idyll—on the subject of the university Act, revived in that year by Aldrich. Six years later the piece was thought worth printing among the *Poemata melioris notae* included in the two volumes of *Musarum Anglicarum Analecta*; where it is preceded by a poem of Aldrich's and followed by a poem of Addison's. The comedy which he printed in 1703 is, though not particularly witty, not without wit—Betterton and Mrs. Bracegirdle acted in it, George Granville wrote the Epilogue. A sentence from this comedy might have furnished the motto to 'Boyle against Bentley': 'He has one damned ill Quality above all the rest, he speaks well of all Mankind.'

For the publication of his *Phalaris*, Boyle was left to make his own arrangements with the booksellers. Since, in the style of a Man of Quality, he asked no share of the profits, he had no difficulty in finding a printer who was willing to take the risks of printing his book. These were not considerable; Aldrich himself took 100 copies, and nearly the whole of the edition was without difficulty subscribed in Oxford alone. Dedicated to the dean—who happened at the time to be also vice-chancellor—the book appeared ἐκ Θεάτρου ἐν 'Οξονίᾳ on 1 January 1695. The preface contained two notable sentences; of which the first paraphrased the judgement upon Phalaris of 'that great glory of our age and nation', Sir William Temple; the second spoke of the 'singular humanity' of the King's Librarian, who had refused the editor reasonable facilities for collating a manuscript in the Royal Library.

The King's Librarian addressed to the editor a letter of complaint, in which, denying the discourtesy charged against him, 'Perhaps I might think myself obliged', he wrote, 'to make a public vindication.' He was told in reply that 'what he said in his own behalf might be true; but that Mr. Bennet had represented the thing quite otherwise'. Mr. Bennet was the London bookseller through whom Boyle had applied for the use of the manuscript. As for his threat of 'a public vindication', Bentley 'might do himself right in what manner he pleased'.

Bentley had been quick to bark. But it was two years before he saw fit to bite. Though his friends urged him to 'defend the honour' of the King's Librarian, he 'resolv'd to take no notice' of 'the insult', but 'to let the matter drop'. He took this course, he would have us believe, 'out of a natural aversion to all quarrels and broils, and out of regard to the Editor himself'. In 1697, however, a new edition of Wotton's *Reflections* was required. When Wotton was preparing the first, Bentley had promised to contribute to it 'a dissertation about Phalaris and Aesop', but 'could not at that time be as good as his word'. Wotton now asked him to redeem his promise of three years ago. But, in the meantime, Boyle's *Phalaris* had appeared with the 'insult' which Bentley had 'resolv'd to take no notice of'. Bentley, not wishing 'to be necessitated to give an account of that Story', begged to be excused. But Wotton was not the man to take No for an answer; and, forgetting his 'aversion to all quarrels and broils', and his 'regard' for Boyle, Bentley contributed to the new *Reflections* a 'Dissertation upon the Epistles of Phalaris . . . and the Fables of Aesop'.

At the end of the section upon Phalaris, he 'begs the favour of one word' with Phalaris's 'late editors'—the plural, to indicate that Boyle's book is the work, not of himself, but of his tutors. Of his one word, the first four pages are occupied with the 'vindication' of his own behaviour in the matter of the manuscript. There follow ten pages devoted to exposing the faults of scholarship in Boyle's book.

In the quarrel about the manuscript, Bentley's biographers mostly side with Bentley. Monk, De Quincey, Hartley Coleridge, and Jebb do so without hesitation. Hinton, however, Bentley's earliest biographer, is more doubtful. 'The whole', he writes, 'is so perplexed and confounded that there is no coming at the truth and reality of the affair.' For this he makes Bentley himself primarily responsible. Bentley allowed an interval of more than two years to elapse between Boyle's complaint and his answer to it. Between some of the incidents discussed and the discussion of them there is an interval of three years. When Bentley excuses this interval by his 'natural aversion to all quarrels and broils', we are entitled to remember that most of his life, and a great part of his scholarship, was given to quarrels and broils. The explanation of the interval is simpler than this. He had written to Boyle in the first instance on 26 January 1695. The purpose of his letter was, no doubt, as he states it—he hoped that Boyle 'would put a stop to the publication of his Book, till he had altered that Passage' (the 'singular humanity' passage). As late as 1699 he writes that 'it was in his power to stop it . . . he might have cut out the leaf and printed a new one'. In fact, it was not in Boyle's power to stop the book. A hundred copies of it had been given out in Christ Church on 1 January 1695, and by the 25th of the month all the booksellers had their copies.[1] But Bentley had hoped to stop the book; and that failing, he left the matter alone. It put an affront upon him. Yet it is difficult not to think that in this matter of the manuscript he had been, to say the least, unhelpful and peremptory. Bennet could produce correspondence between himself and Boyle which showed that Bentley's assistance had been invoked at least as early as the beginning of October 1693. At that date Bentley was not yet King's Librarian; but he was applied to because he was in a position to assist. On his own showing he did nothing until the end of the second week in May 1694. On a day which he calculates to have been either the 13th or the 14th of that month, he delivered the manuscript to Bennet. According to his own account he stipulated that it should be returned on 19 May. Bennet, however, denied that any date was named for its return. Five days, in any case, did not allow Bennet much time to find a collator, nor the collator much time to do his work. But on 19 May Bentley demanded the return of the manuscript; and to Bennet's request that the collator might retain it till the following

[1] *A Short Account of Dr. Bentley's Humanity*, &c., p. 121.

morning gave a brusque refusal: he was going out of town on 21 May, and did not see why he should be at the trouble of going to the library on 20 May, which was a Sunday. The collator had collated the first forty chapters—the afternoon of 19 May gave him plenty of time, Bentley said, to do the eighty-seven remaining chapters. 'For experiment's sake' Bentley himself collated the first forty chapters, and found that it took him an hour and eighteen minutes. The first forty chapters in Boyle's text make 400 lines. Bentley's rate of collation is, accordingly, something above five lines to the minute. It is difficult to believe that any modern scholar would think this a safe rate, even for the collation of a printed text in English. Bentley's zeal for the safety of this manuscript seems, in any case, somewhat exaggerated, when we remember that he thought himself entitled to keep the Codex Alexandrinus—perhaps the most important manuscript in the world—in his own lodgings.

Bentley, then, was not helpful. Nor had he been at pains to conceal his contempt for the project of editing Phalaris. 'It was my hard hap', he writes, 'to say the Epistles of Phalaris were spurious, and unworthy of a new edition.' It was, no doubt, his 'hard hap' to be reported with additions; and there is perhaps something in his suggestion that Bennet used misrepresentation in order to cover up 'his own neglect'. But sufficient had passed to hurt Boyle's pride; and he was young enough to enjoy writing the sentence about Bentley's 'singular humanity'. The sarcasm is only effective if we suppose that the repute of Bentley's discourtesy was already fairly general.

The ten pages in which Bentley reviews the faults of

Boyle's edition are not a favourable specimen of his scholarship; and he was probably conscious of this, for he omits them from the second edition of his *Dissertation.* Except that he convicts Boyle of having in two places overlooked a true reading of the manuscripts, the criticisms which he makes are not telling—to any one of them it would be possible to devise a plausible rejoinder. Of his 'singular humanity' he could not have given a more unfortunate illustration. Boyle was a youth of twenty. On a tolerable construction of it, his offence was not much more than a schoolboy pleasantry. But so roughly did the first scholar in Europe handle this pert undergraduate that he enlisted half the world on the side of 'Boyle against Bentley'. 'A severe critic sowr'd into a fit of unmannerly Rage, against an innocent Gentleman'; 'a Mean Dull Unmannerly Pedant'—expressions like these, devised by Bentley's enemies, found an easy and winning career.

Bentley himself gave to our language the word Phalarism. 'There's a certain Temper of Mind that Cicero calls Phalarism, A Spirit like Phalaris's.' 'One would be apt to imagine', he adds, impudently, 'that a Portion of it had descended upon some of his Translators.' As a method of scholarship, what he calls 'the Science of Phalarism' has, in fact, for its foremost practitioners, in Latin Scaliger and Salmasius, in English Bentley and Housman.

The main body of the *Dissertation* is occupied with the proof of the spuriousness of the letters attributed to Phalaris. Whether disingenuously or from mere carelessness, Bentley has forgotten to tell the reader that Boyle himself, in the preface to his edition, had questioned the genuineness of the letters. More than that: Boyle had put to the reader some of Bentley's own arguments, stating them briefly and sensibly, putting first the argument which Bentley himself puts first, that, namely, which derives from the dialect in which they are written. It is not more than good sport when later, in *Boyle against Bentley*, he indicates that Bentley's reasons for supposing the letters spurious have half converted him to a faith in their genuineness. I think we may believe him when he tells us that he edited the letters because he enjoyed them—he found in them 'life and smartness'. That Temple should have enjoyed them is more remarkable, at least for the reason given by Boyle, when he writes that: 'Sir William Temple has spent a good part of his Life in transacting Affairs of State; He has written to Kings, and They to Him; and this has qualified him to judge how Kings should write.' The truth is that knowledge of the world does not help a man to detect literary imposture. Nobody, again, ever knew so well how kings talked as Shakespeare, who had never the opportunity of conversing with them.

Bentley had intimated covertly that Boyle's edition was the work of his tutors. In the preface to *Boyle against Bentley*, Boyle gives an account of the matter which is frank and natural and may pass for true. But of *Boyle against Bentley* it is pretty certain that he wrote little more than the preface and the first twenty-nine pages (those that deal with the question of the manuscript). Warburton had it, on the authority of Pope, that 'the body of the criticism' was the work of Atterbury and (John) Freind. The 'droll argument' by which Bentley is proved not to be the author of the

Dissertation was supplied by King. So, too, was the telling index. Other accounts name other auxiliaries—Smalridge, Alsop, Robert Freind. The presiding genius of the undertaking was Atterbury. It seems to have escaped the notice of the commentators that Wotton, who had introduced Bentley's *Dissertation* to the world, was rector of the parish[1] in which Atterbury was born, succeeding Atterbury's father. It is worth noting, again, that a niece of Freind's became Bentley's daughter-in-law.

Boyle against Bentley was at any rate first-class journalism. Nor did it lack a kind of learning. Its authors were not fools, and they had not been lazy—they had rummaged widely in antiquity. If now their scholarship seems despicable, it must be remembered that they were pitted against Bentley. If they were beaten, perhaps nobody knew it except Bentley and themselves. Boyle had the wit to suspect it—rather basely, he blamed Atterbury. 'They have had enough of me', Bentley wrote in 1706, 'and hereafter will let me alone.' But they had the world with them—the only sure test of good journalism. Garth's preposterous *mot* expressed the world's judgement—'to a Bentley 'tis we owe a Boyle'. The wit of *Boyle against Bentley* is good. The

[1] Milton Keynes, near Bletchley. In Foster's *Alumni* Wotton has become confused with his namesake William Wotton of St. John's, Oxford; and to the latter are assigned not only the living of the former, but his wife and children and degrees. The St. John's Wotton was a friend of Smalridge. Smalridge introduced him to Atterbury as 'an honest warm fellow'. Rumour said that he had been expelled from St. John's for drinking the health of the Devil (*Epistolary Correspondence of F. Atterbury*, i, pp. 7–9). In the Bodleian is a letter of his to Archbishop Sancroft, through whom he seeks to obtain a fellowship at St. John's (I owe my knowledge of the letter to Mr. J. A. W. Bennett).

scholarship is not good; but it was good enough for the purpose. Its badness was of a kind that made an effective exposure of it difficult. There was an infinite parade of learned detail, of which nearly every item was vitiated by inaccuracy. Bentley's prime embarrassment was that he had to handle a succession of errors of minute detail. He was driven upon detail and minuteness; he had to fight, that is, upon ground where it was difficult to be victorious without being dull and tiresome. Yet to be dull and tiresome was to be beaten—it was to give his enemies just what they wanted, and to earn the title of 'Pedant'. Perhaps not all the means by which Bentley saved his *Dissertation* from dullness are creditable—some of the most effective writing in it has no better inspiration than 'unmannerly rage'. But, whatever the faults of his book, no other book in the world is at once so learned and so little dull.

To Boyle, in truth—or to *Boyle against Bentley*—we owe, not a Bentley merely, but two Bentleys: the scholar, and the wit. And yet they are not two persons, but one; the embodiment of a single quality, deadly accuracy of mind.

Bentley's *Dissertation* is one of the grand monuments of European scholarship. Something like a century had passed since Scaliger had given to the world his *Emendatio Temporum*, with its great sequel the *Thesaurus*. With those two books Scaliger broke down the barrier between secular and religious learning, altering for ever the whole horizon of scholarship. With them learning achieves untrammelled outlook, beholding in one equal view east and west, the near and the distant. How much of modern learning has its forgotten source in them, it would be difficult to say. Today they are scarcely read, even by scholars. Yet we use them in all our studies, we use them as we use air and the light, with little thought of the genius which built the firmament and divided the darkness from the day. Bentley's *Dissertation* is not a book of such universal character. Yet the sweep and range of it, though less catholic, is wide and deep. There still lives in it something of the temper of the heroical age of scholarship. When all is said and done, Bentley's heart was with that heroical age; it would be a mistake to allow his 'wit', and the element of blackguardism in him, to obscure his fundamental seriousness in the construction of truth. On a personal matter he was perhaps not always truthful. But in scholarship he was scrupulously truthful. His book lives by qualities deeper than those for which it is read.

It is read for its readability, its versatility, its modernity; and because it has the luck of being written in the vernacular, and connects with Temple and Swift and the rise of modern science. If it is not literature, it rubs shoulders with literature. It is the only great work of scholarship which is read by persons who are not scholars. It is the only book in the world from which a man who is not a scholar can get to know what great scholarship means.

By the time Bentley's book appeared, Temple was dead. His whole connexion with this 'battle of the books' had been paradoxical. The strife of tongues was essentially distasteful to him. He had given the signal for the onset by an inadvertence. He had not blown a trumpet-call; he had dropped an aside. Hating whatsoever things are even mildly vulgar, it had fallen to him to be the invisible headquarters of a war waged with all the weapons of vulgarity. In a strife waged for Greek, and about Greek, and to a large extent in Greek, he did not know Greek. He knew his own likes and dislikes. He liked the ancients, and he disliked the moderns. His natural friends were the scholars, his natural enemies Gresham House and modern science. In the event he found himself opposed by the greatest scholar whom this country has produced. Yet harder was it to bear, that of the many persons who engaged themselves in the controversy, Wotton, who represented Gresham House, was the only one who wrote like a gentleman. Temple was, again, a Cambridge man; he had dedicated his book to the University of Cambridge. Yet Wotton and Bentley were Cambridge men; the support of Temple's cause had to be entrusted to Oxford.

Swift may perhaps be called an Oxford man by accident. He had taken a Dublin degree 'by special favour'—a term used, says Dr. Johnson, in that university 'to denote want of merit'. But the University of Oxford granted him the degree of M.A., in the belief (if we may credit Orrery) that the Dublin phrase 'by special favour' 'signified a degree conferred in reward of extraordinary diligence or learning'. Swift entered the battle when it was, in effect, over; not, it seems likely, from loyalty to Temple, or from love of a losing side; but with something of the instinct of the vulture.

REFERENCE-BOOKS

BAYLE AND HIS DICTIONARY

NOBODY now reads Bayle's Dictionary, for its values have been subsumed into a changed human life—if we live at liberty to think, and to say what we think, we stand indebted, in large part, to Bayle. Nobody reads the Dictionary, and nobody is much interested in Bayle. The life of Bayle is, in truth, bookish. The man is his Dictionary. Sainte-Beuve tried to find a mistress for him; and Brunetière has no doubt that, if it could be done, Bayle and Baylism would be interesting again. Meantime, 'I do not think,' writes Brunetière, 'that in the whole history of literature anybody has ever been treated so unjustly and ungratefully as Bayle.' The truth is, he does not belong to literature. He influenced literature profoundly. But he is, in fact, a second-rate writer. Has he been worse treated than Darwin? Are we particularly unjust to Darwin, or ungrateful, if, today, no one reads *The Origin of Species*, no one finds the life of Darwin exciting?

Really, has Bayle much to complain of? Did ever a Dictionary have the luck of his? 'Do you think', he writes to Du Rondel, 'that a great moral good cannot result from a critical Dictionary?' Du Rondel was a Professor of Philology; and he probably went to dictionaries for something different. Bayle's Dictionary was, none the less, a great moral instrument. The Bible of Voltaire, and Frederick the Great, and all atheists, it did, in fact, make men better. We have become so much better by it that we hardly need it. In 1765 Frederick the Great published a two-volume selection from it. Today a less princely selection may suffice. Mr. Beller and Mr. Lee have edited for the Princeton University Press a selection in one volume.[1] The selection is well made. Room, even so, might have been found for extracts from Bayle's 1692 'Dissertation', from the 1697 preface, and from some of the 1702 'Explanations'—all these appear in the earliest English translation. The introduction prefixed to the selection is competent, and sufficiently conventional. The text offered may be styled 'bothering'. It incorporates in Bayle's text Bayle's immense footnotes (the footnotes being distinguished by square brackets). This may well be thought to consult the convenience of the printer rather than the reader. But the book is a useful enterprise. It will perform a service if it makes us ask what need Bayle's Dictionary was set to satisfy, what quality constitutes the miracle and mystery of it.

The Dictionary is not what it was meant to be when Bayle first began work upon it. In May 1692 he designed 'to compose a Dictionary of Errors', 'the perfection of which was to consist in observing all mistakes, great or small', that were to be found in other people's dictionaries. As if that were not enough, he proposed to diversify his

[1] *Selections from Bayle's Dictionary*. Edited by E. A. Beller and M. du P Lee, Jr., 1953.

work by 'making sallies upon all sorts of authors, wherever occasion offers'. Specimens of this Dictionary of Errors were issued, it would seem, to a somewhat apathetic public. Bayle became aware that people who read books care very little about the mistakes in them; and 'the better to adapt myself to the public taste,' he writes, 'I changed my plan.' He persuaded himself before long, or professed to have done so, that the public taste was truer than his own. In the preface to the first edition of his Dictionary, 'it is certain', he says, 'that the discovery of errors is not important to the prosperity of the state, or of private persons'. It is all as cynical as could be. But it was no good offering the public a Dictionary that would not sell.

The public did not want a Dictionary of Errors. They were quite right; and they should have something else. In July of 1692 Bayle began on the Dictionary that we have, delivering the goods in October 1696.

> Observe now [he writes in 1696] in what manner I have changed my plan. . . . I have divided my composition into two parts. One is purely historical, and gives a succinct account of matters of fact. The other is a large commentary, a miscellany of proofs and discussions, wherein I have inserted a censure of many faults, and sometimes a train of philosophical reflections; in a word, there is variety enough to presume that all sorts of readers will find something or other that will please them.

The whole bears the title *Dictionnaire Historique et Critique*. It is, we may suspect, a good deal more like the Dictionary that the public did *not* want than the public supposed. A Dictionary of Errors could hardly catalogue more errors;

nor could any dictionary be more fertile of 'sallies'. Certainly, 'variety' has been studied. Certainly, 'all sorts of readers' have been catered for. The Rotterdam Consistory complained of the plethora of obscene matter collected in the Dictionary. ' 'Tis a subject', Bayle wrote, 'more difficult to treat than one can think.' But he brings to it some sense and a good deal of ingenuity.

Of the original Dictionary of Errors 'the principal design' was 'to observe the faults of Moreri'. Whatever Moreri's faults, they did not much hinder his vogue. His Dictionary was first published in 1674. It owed something to Charles Stephens's *Historical, Geographical and Poetical Dictionary*, the earliest of the encyclopaedias, if we except that of Gesner. In 1670 Stephens's Dictionary (of which there had been as many as four editions) was revised by an Oxford scholar, Nicholas Lloyd. It was Lloyd whom Moreri utilized, putting him quickly out of account. Moreri, when Bayle took him in hand, had already achieved five editions in France and two in Holland. The Dutch editions Bayle goes out of his way to praise—the editor was Le Clerc, and he had accommodated Moreri to Protestant tastes. When he wrote his 1697 preface Bayle had heard rumours of an English translation of Moreri. The English Moreri, in fact, appeared in 1694. The translators, good Protestants, were careful to advertise the reader that what they offered was Le Clerc's Moreri. A second edition of the book, carrying Jeremy Collier's name as editor, was printed in 1701 (the *Cambridge Bibliography* and the *Cambridge History of English Literature* need correcting here).

But what life was left in the English Moreri petered out

when, in 1710, the first English Bayle appeared—of the book in French the sales in England, the translators tell us, had been very great. Moreri was full of mistakes. Mistakes, Bayle says, do no great harm, unless they are mistakes in religion. Moreri made the mistake of being a Roman Catholic, and letting his reader know it. A 'controversist' Bayle calls him—'this is one of his greatest faults', he says; 'in a dictionary, nothing is more ridiculous'. For himself, he undertakes to 'use the same liberty towards authors of all nations and religions'; and a fine impartiality informs, in truth, his captious book. One can be impartial, perhaps, about anything if one is positive about nothing. From a dictionary, an encyclopaedia, one looks for information. One hopes for truth. Bayle is endlessly informative. And 'I advance nothing', he writes, 'as truth when I am persuaded that it is falsity.' But 'I am sometimes', he adds, 'more positive than I should be. Yet at the bottom I only propose doubts.' The amount of good information that his Dictionary furnished, particularly biographical information, made it a necessary book. Dr. Johnson would hear nothing against Bayle's Lives. 'Mr. McLean said, he had a confutation of Bayle by Leibniz.—*Johnson* "A confutation of Bayle, Sir! The greatest part of his writings is not confutable; it is historical and critical."' Bayle furnished, in a hundred directions, useful information. Even so, it was 'by proposing doubts' that he won the world. 'Is it not the very nerve of prudence', he asks, in a footnote (citing Epicharmus), 'not to believe too hastily?' Indeed, he should have blazoned the title-page of his Dictionary with Epicharmus's *μέμνασ' ἀπιστεῖν*.

It is difficult to know what Bayle did in fact believe in. If he believed in God, he did not believe, or he pretended not to believe, in arguing about Him. 'It is for the metaphysicians', he writes, 'to examine whether there be a God. But Christians, as Christians, ought to suppose it a thing already determined.' That is from the 'Explanation concerning the Sceptics', printed with the 1702 Dictionary.

> You must necessarily take an option [he goes on] between philosophy and the Gospel. If you will believe nothing but what is evident and agreeable to common notions, choose philosophy. If you will believe the incomprehensible mysteries of religion, take Christianity and leave philosophy; for to possess evidence and incomprehensibility together is a thing impossible.

So he reasons with the Protestant Consistory of Rotterdam, who found sceptical matter in what he had written about Pyrrho. Incidentally, he sees no more reason, he tells his critics, for excluding sceptical matter from his Dictionary than for excluding obscene matter—a dictionary must be readable. A recent volume of essays, *The French Mind*—an Oxford offering to Professor Rudler—contains an essay on Bayle by Mr. W. H. Barber. It is a mistake, Mr. Barber thinks, to call Bayle a sceptic. But it is a mistake which everyone has made, till Mr. Barber. Bayle, for Mr. Barber, is an orthodox Calvinist. For a brief space he was an orthodox Catholic. But he found truth at the last, or even earlier. Did he, in fact, seek it, or very much love it? Did he not, rather, all his life, and in all his writings, love before all things dialectic?

Bayle may have believed in God. But certainly he did not believe in Man. 'Man', he says, 'is an incorrigible animal; he is as wicked to-day as in the first centuries.' A man is none the worse, even so, for being an atheist. Atheism, Bayle affirms, 'does not necessarily conduct to corruption of morals'. Experience, indeed, shows that a knowledge of God does not correct a man's vicious inclinations. 'You may call Man a reasonable creature to your heart's content; it remains true, none the less,' says Bayle, 'that he almost never acts according to his principles.' The eighteenth-century *philosophes* did not like all of this. They liked freedom of belief, they liked toleration. They liked a man to think for himself, unfettered. But they liked it for a reason which they did not find in Bayle. They liked it because they believed in Man. 'The *Encyclopédie*', it has been said, 'is nothing else than a revised and enlarged edition of Bayle's Dictionary.' That needs heavy qualification. The Encyclopaedists believed in Man. They believed in Man, and in the progress of Man: a progress conditioned by reason and science. Bayle believed not so much in reason as in reasoning. For science he had, and expressed, a healthy contempt. A principal aim of the Dictionary of Errors, he tells Du Rondel, is to give men 'a true notion of the emptiness and vanity of the sciences'. If he writes, later, that 'the discovery of errors is not important' to people, or peoples, he finds it, none the less, entertaining. The Dictionary will do something if it helps to 'mortify man in respect to his greatest vanity, I mean his science'.

The first volume of the *Encyclopédie* appeared in 1751; the thirty-five volumes of it were completed in 1780: 'a reasoned Dictionary of Sciences, Arts and Crafts' (so the title-page designates it). Lloyd, Moreri, Bayle could not help with the sciences. Lloyd and Moreri are dictionaries 'historical, geographical, and poetical'. Bayle is 'historical and critical'—was ever dictionary quite so critical? In search of the sciences the Encyclopaedists, or their publisher, went to an English dictionary which, except that they used it, nobody today would want to look at; but a dictionary succinct and businesslike, the *Cyclopaedia* of Ephraim Chambers; 'an Universal Dictionary of Arts and Sciences'. Yet, not Chambers made their Dictionary, but Bayle. 'Beyond a doubt', says Brunetière, 'it was in the writings of Bayle that Montesquieu, Voltaire, Diderot, Rousseau, Helvétius—to say nothing of lesser men—learned to read, to reason, to think.' To Mr. Beller and Mr. Lee Voltaire is Bayle's 'greatest pupil'. 'It was he', they tell us, 'who carried on Bayle's work with such an abundance of pyrotechnics as to eclipse his master.' 'Intolerably intelligible', Voltaire calls Bayle; . . . 'he puts even those of the most meagre understanding in a position to judge, and even to doubt, what is told them.' Bayle's Dictionary taught men to think for themselves; it insisted on the liberty of every man to do so. What might come of it, who should say?—that was not Bayle's business. The Encyclopaedists took Man more seriously. They believed in his corrigibility, his perfectibility. They brought to the study of him, what in all his studies Bayle lacked, enthusiasm.

In Bayle's Dictionary, says a friendly French critic of it, you may find everything except what you are looking for.

When Dr. Johnson went to his Bayle, what biographies did he seek? Of English names there are not much above thirty. Milton is there. But of our other poets there is none—unless we are to count George Buchanan, who was interesting to Bayle rather for his Lutheranism than his poetry. The philosophers do a little better. Roger Bacon is there; and Francis Bacon. Hobbes is there. It might be expected that this Cartesian would have something to say about Newton. But no word is there about Newton; nor any word about Descartes either. It is interesting to find Bayle quoting Sir Thomas Browne's *Religio Medici*. But there is no biography of Browne. With the ancients he is as capricious as with the moderns. There is plenty about Aristotle. But nothing about Plato. Greek poetry is represented by Euripides and Simonides. But Aeschylus and Sophocles might never have lived; or Pindar either. Homer may have been one poet or several. Bayle knows none of them. The Latins do a little better. Even so, the Dictionary knows not Cicero.

Bayle's preface makes all sorts of excuses for the omission of this or that. But not much of what he says is plausible. The truth is, he liked pleasing himself. And he liked displeasing other people. The Dictionary is before all else a disquieting book. To surprise, to irritate, to scandalize—all this for Bayle was an essential part of criticism. He made himself felt. He is felt still. But not remembered; or if remembered, remembered for his influence upon greater men—men who, using what he gave them, reshaped the world.

THE CONCISE *C.H.E.L.*

A thousand pages in my sight are not properly called a concise book.[1] But Mr. Sampson found that he was enjoying himself; and again and again 'concise be damned', he says plainly. I do not know what the Cambridge Press intended. But I know what Mr. Sampson did not intend. He did not intend just to 'boil down' the *C.H.E.L.* Nor merely to 'hot it up' (though his literary cuisine affects sometimes the piquant and peppery). He intended to write his own book; and to make it, what almost everywhere it is, fresh and readable. I say 'almost everywhere', for Mr. Sampson is sometimes perfunctory on purpose. There is a good deal of the *C.H.E.L.* which has nothing to do with literature, properly considered; and Mr. Sampson is, before all else, set to consider literature properly. The nineteenth-century philosophers bore him; so do the scientists; so do the nineteenth-century historians, excepting Macaulay, and perhaps Froude. The first two parts, accordingly, of his fourteenth chapter are perfunctory. If I like him the better for it, it is because I like partisanship, and the froudacious. If he could have had his own way, Mr. Sampson, I suspect, would have left out half the book. It would then have been Concise; but perhaps rather more Oxford than Cambridge. Every now and again, in truth, Mr. Sampson does leave out almost everything. Most of his life he has been mixed up with Education; and when, in the ninth volume of the *C.H.E.L.*, he comes to

[1] *The Concise Cambridge History of English Literature*, by George Sampson, 1941.

chapter xv (Education, from Cromwell to George II), it is more than he can bear; and he reduces its forty-four pages to twenty-seven lines. There are other sections where excision would have served his turn better than concision. In section 15 of his twelfth chapter he is plainly bored with Nineteenth-century Scholars, and frankly perfunctory. What has Mayor's Juvenal to do with English literature? Or Nettleship's *Contributions to Latin Lexicography*? Why list Jebb—'the accomplished editor of Sophocles . . . and the eloquent *author* of *The Attic Orators*'? Of Robinson Ellis he says (I think justly) that his metrical version of Catullus 'has many true touches of poetry'. Ellis himself had none. I like the malice with which our classical archaeology is carried back to the Society of Dilettanti. But the whole section could well have been omitted.

It is when the *C.H.E.L. stops* that Mr. Sampson really gets going. The ninety pages on late-Victorian and post-Victorian Literature are all his own; and none the worse for that. Some of the persons mentioned in them will not much like what is said of them. Some who are not mentioned at all will like that even less. For myself, I liked this chapter above all, thinking the whole of it a spirited and competent performance. Many of the writers spoken of I have never read; and I now know that I need not. With most of Mr. Sampson's judgements I find myself, where I am able to judge at all, in hearty agreement; especially with the sharp ones. But I must still ask, if Mr. T. S. Eliot is as bad as all that, why must Mr. Sampson give more space to him than he allows to Lamb, to Landor, to de Quincey, to Jane Austen? Where he must be sharp, let him be short. He is short and sharp, to my mind preposterously, with Rupert Brooke: concise unkindness could no further go. But all of us have our blind spots; and I will not bother my head about it. *μαρτυρήσει χρόνος*. I give Mr. Sampson particularly good marks for his generous appreciation of the poetry of Gilbert Murray, and for his detraction of Murray's detractors. If it is a sin not to be like Euripides, Murray is an offending soul, and must answer for it to Posterity. But Posterity has a way of liking the readable.

I am sufficiently touched with time to like, in literature, nothing else; and no longer to read unreadable books. Of whatsoever things in English literature are readable, Mr. Sampson's book furnishes the most readable history that I have met. Its only rival I should suppose to be Saintsbury's *Short History*. Saintsbury I must esteem a great man, but a bad writer. Mr. Sampson writes very well—i.e. so that he can be read. I do not suppose that he has Saintsbury's multifarious first-hand learning. But he has, at second-hand, the multifarious composite learning of the *C.H.E.L.* —the less of it he uses, the better I like his book. His best quality he shares with Saintsbury—a gift of telling summary. The outstanding things stand out. Nails are hit on the head. Heads are broken gentlemanlike. Men and books jostle one another happily. The true and the interesting are not too fussily distinguished.

Sometimes Mr. Sampson is in a hurry. He calls *David Copperfield* 'one of the few really great English novels'. As though our literature were not richer in great fiction than any other; as though we did not groan with great novels; as though, after Shakespeare, there was anything like it anywhere in the world. On p. 575 he says that 'nearly all that is supremely great in Wordsworth's poetry' belongs to the years 1798–1805. But two pages later he censures as 'uncritical' 'the stock objection that nothing published after the volumes of 1807 matters very much'. But I would not take too heavily occasional signs of haste. To be in a hurry is at least one way of getting on. And Mr. Sampson does get on; and he gets *somewhere*; never losing heart in a task which must sometimes have tried his patience. With a title that doomed him to look second-hand, he has succeeded in being first-hand and first-rate. He is never uninteresting, except on purpose; and upon the authors that matter he abounds in good and pure criticism.

It did not surprise me to read the other day a letter, in (I think) *The Times Literary Supplement*, suggesting that the time had now come to make all the Cambridge Histories concise. *Sampsonise the lot!* There is a good deal to be said for it; if there are Sampsons enough to go round, or if Mr. George Sampson will go round. But it is disquieting to reflect how few books there are in the world which could not be made better by being made concise.

C.B.E.L.

This[1] is a great book. It did not need the blurb to tell me that 'no one man' could have made it. It has in fact been made by as many as 190 men, with Mr. F. W. Bateson standing over them, I will not say with a stick, but (to use his own words) 'with stubborn insistence', 'checking and

[1] *The Cambridge Bibliography of English Literature*, edited by F. W. Bateson, 1940.

revising the majority of the sections' himself. I should like to think that, on the day on which they rested from their labours, these 190 bibliographers dined together, forgiving one another's shortcomings, and not exchanging information. 'No one man', says the blurb, 'is likely ever to need all the information that this book contains.' I should hope not. It contains a record, for the period 600–1900, of the authors, titles, and editions of all books, English and Latin, which have any literary interest, written by 'natives of what is now the British Empire'. It contains, in addition, a record of 'secondary books and articles', dealing with the biography and criticism of the primary authors catalogued. The record of biographical and critical material is particularly valuable; the more so as it is brought down to 1935 (and for the third volume down to 1938). The record of primary books purports, so far as they still possess any 'literary interest', to be complete (Preface, p. i), though a later paragraph introduces important qualifications. That of secondary books is necessarily selective; and the varying quality of the 190 contributors is pleasantly illustrated by what they omit or include. In general, 'no type of printed book, from the chapbook to the scientific treatise, from the collection of hymns to the gift-book, from the schoolboy's "crib" to the treatise on whist, had been altogether neglected'. Whist appears in the section *Literature of Sport*: where, however, I was disappointed not to find bridge. Can I be wrong in thinking that *The Pocket Guide to Bridge* by Boaz goes back to the early nineties? Another disappointment was in connexion with the subject of shorthand. Mr. Bateson calls his book a 'shorthand history of English

Literature'; and for this and other reasons I was curious to see how the history of shorthand fared in the *C.B.E.L.* It fares ill—unless I have missed something, the history of shorthand ends, for the *C.B.E.L.*, in the eighteenth century. Sir Isaac Pitman is honourably mentioned among publishers; but of his connexions with shorthand *οὐδὲ γρῦ*.

I say 'unless I have missed something'. For the truth is that it is not always easy to know what is, or is not, to be found in this book. It deserved a better index. That it should index, not books, but authors was perhaps necessary. It gives the titles of books only for anonymous works; though even here there is no complete consistency. The author of *Supernatural Religion* took so much pains to conceal his name that very few people in fact know it. But his book can be found, in this index, only by somebody who happens to remember that he was called Cassels, or that his contentions were laboriously refuted by Lightfoot. The index is to some extent a subject-index as well as an author-index. But so taken, it offers many perplexities. I found *whist*, as I say, in the section *Literature of Sport*. But by sheer good luck; for neither under *sport* nor under *whist* is it indexed. For all Mr. Bateson's profession of kindness, again, towards schoolboys' 'cribs', I cannot find indexed those old friends of my boyhood, Kelly's Keys. I wanted to know something about the *Biographia Britannica*. But it is not indexed—among the Lives in it is a Life of Bentley which deserved mention among the 'secondary books' about that scholar (as did the Life by Hartley Coleridge). *Biographia Britannica* is not indexed. The *Encyclopaedia Britannica* is not indexed. I wished for some information about Thomas

Astle's *Origin and Progress of Writing*. Neither under *Astle* nor under *Writing* nor under *Handwriting* could I discover anything at all. I am not complaining of what is not in the book; but of what is certainly there, but buried, for want of adequate indexing. I have said what a valuable part of the book is the record of 'secondary books and articles'. It is a real misfortune that no attempt has been made to index these beyond the year 1870. It is a misfortune, again, that 'foreign writers are normally omitted altogether' from the index.

The 190 contributors deserved, themselves, to be better indexed. Mr. Bateson believes himself (Preface, p. viii) to have given a complete list of them at the beginning of the first volume. A complete list of them is, in truth, nowhere to be found. My figure of 190 is arrived at by a comparison of three separate lists, one for each volume. Some of the contributors are so learned that they contribute to all three volumes (a shining example is Mr. H. G. Pollard). My 190 involved a process of addition and subtraction so tiresome that, if I have got the sum wrong, I refuse to take the blame. There should have been a single list; and it should have given, against the name of each contributor, the sections of the work for which he is responsible. Or, if this was too difficult, it would have been easy, in the tables of contents at the beginning of each volume, to give, for each section, the name or initials of the writer. As it is, to be sure that I have overlooked nothing, say, of Mr. Pollard's, I am obliged, literally, to turn three-thousand-odd pages of text; and when I have done it I have no surety that I have not missed his initials at the end of some shy sub-section. Often enough, it is true, turning the pages, I can guess who is who from the quality of the work. Mr. Pollard's quality is unmistakable. His account of News-sheets and Newspapers from 1500 to 1900 is an outstanding achievement. If the Prime Minister had been primed by Mr. Pollard, he would have known better than to congratulate *Berrow's Worcester Journal* on its 250th birthday.

Two other challenging performances in this Bibliography I will allow myself to mention. The one is Mr. Ault's article on the Poetical Miscellanies of the seventeenth and eighteenth centuries; the other Mr. Raby's account of the Latin Writers of the Anglo-Saxon and Middle English periods.

Regretfully I leave unsung the other 187 heroes of this memorable enterprise. To express their merits would require at least 187 reviewers; and the things that they have done amiss they will hear about soon enough from all the world. Perhaps without discourtesy to any of them I may suggest that some of the Introductions to sections are too general and 'airy'; that the classifications which they offer are limp, and that, endeavouring to give 'background', they create mist.

In a book like this we all look, I suppose, to see what is said about our friends. It is so that I happened to notice that from the list of F. H. Bradley's works the posthumous *Aphorisms* is missing; from that of W. A. Raleigh's, the play *James* (Oxford, 1913), which Raleigh sometimes spoke of as 'the finest thing he had ever written' (it is not really very good). It amused me that Robinson Ellis should figure only as a minor poet—with a note, however, to the effect that his most important work was his Commentary on Catullus. A reference to 'Rev. D. Nichol Smith' bothered me—by sheer cleverness I tumbled to it that 'Rev.' meant 'revised by' (for which elsewhere I find both 'rev.' and '*rev.*' used). I mention this because, in general, the book would have been easier to use if the printer had allowed himself a greater variety of type.

MILTON INDEXED

All indexes are good, even the not very good ones. They sometimes cost a great deal to buy—this particular Index[1] costs four guineas. But they save time, which is money, and which, even if it were not money, would be valuable. They assist us to be accurate, and even to appear learned, without trouble to ourselves. Occasionally, they teach virtue—Cruden's *Concordance* has helped to make men better for two centuries. They proceed invariably from a good, and even innocent, disposition. Of the Index to the Columbia Milton the editor says, I am sure truly, that 'its making has been a strenuous task' and 'a labour of love'. The book, he explains, 'has the external form of a concordance, but it is far from being one. It makes no claim to completeness; not all Milton's words are indexed, though the more important ones appear. Neither are all the places listed in which any one word occurs.' If I understand rightly either the book or the preface, Mr. Patterson's primary concern has been to index, not Milton's words, but his ideas. It is these, he writes, 'that challenge the primary interest of most of us'.

[1] *An Index to the Columbia Edition of the Works of John Milton*, 1940.

In this Index the word *God* occupies ninety-nine columns. These exhibit no paragraphing; there are no headings or sub-headings; no sort of classification is attempted; Milton's uses of the word are set down merely in the order in which they occur in the successive volumes of the Columbia edition of his Works; and when the reader has got to the end, he has to remind himself that the catalogue 'makes no claim to completeness'. I should be sorry to index any man's idea of God—even with a succinct document like the Athanasian Creed, I should feel embarrassed. Yet I believe I could have done something better for Milton than this. Milton's own name occupies a modest thirty columns—and begins after this fashion: 'Milton, John, heart faithful, fearless, steadfast; kindly, genial, tactful; adamant of self confidence; safe from envies and doubts of vulgar; covetous of genius and lofty worth, of sounding lyre, of Muses i. 58 (S 6, 2 *ff.*).' I believe I could have done better than that too.

'For the purposes of condensation' the Index occasionally resorts to paraphrase. But it should do so, surely, only when necessity drives. When Milton writes, and the Columbia editors print, '*beheld A Beavie* of fair Women' (*PL*. xi. 581–2), what necessity drove the indexer to the inexact '*bevy, saw a b.* of fair women'?

To the poetical works of Milton there exist already two 'complete concordances' and unless they were going to improve upon these, the Columbia editors would have done better to leave Milton's verse alone altogether. I can discover nowhere upon what principle they include some words belonging to Milton's poetical vocabulary and exclude others. Why may I not know, for example, that Milton uses the words *agate*, *bleating*, *disinthrone*, *frith*; that he speaks of *day's garish eye* and the *gadding vine*? The omissions I note are taken purely at random. There are plenty of others, and I find most of them unintelligible. 'For Latin poetry the line of the Latin text is given.' I looked up the remarkable word *strato*, which appears as an iambus on the last page of the first part of the volume devoted to the *Minor Poems*. I failed to find it; perhaps because it was an editorial conjecture. 'For Latin prose the references are to the translation.' If the translations were good ones, it would not be easy to defend this. But some of them are notoriously bad—vols. xi and xii, for example, bristle with inexcusable and unbelievable errors. Some of these errors, I am pleased to note, are tacitly corrected in the Index. 'Pole comments correctly on Plato's Gorgias' is a notably incorrect rendering of the Latin 'recte Polus apud Platonem in Gorgia'. In the Index a proper distinction is now made between the Platonic Polus and Cardinal Pole.

However, here are 'two large volumes containing more than 170,000 entries'. It is the devil's plenty; and yet incomplete. So far as Milton's verse is concerned, the editors had a perfectly simple task. They have discharged it, I cannot but think, with some levity. With the prose they had a difficult, it may be an impossible, job. They have brought to it much courage, indeed too much; and a devotion rigorous and entire. Yet, though I have called all indexes good, I must esteem this one not more than a mixed blessing.

With these index-volumes the editors of the Columbia

Milton bring to its conclusion one of the most ambitious critical undertakings of our time. One star differs from another in glory, and of the eighteen volumes of the series, some are good, some (to speak frankly) bad. In respect of all of them special praise should be given to the printer; but as he is Mr. W. E. Rudge, to praise him is perhaps superfluous.

CHRISTIAN NAMES

In this England of ours, Christian names, like Christians, are often oddly remote from Christianity. Twenty per cent. of the children born in Tottenham in 1938 were christened after film-stars. If they had been born in France the law would have seen to it that they were christened either after saints or after 'persons known in ancient history'. If I could be born again, I am not sure that I would not rather be called *Gary* or *Shirley* than *Achilles* or *Aristides.* I should have Miss Withycombe against me.[1] She dislikes our 'neologisms'. Dating her preface 'St. Frideswide's Day' —in Tottenham, we should say 'October 19th'—1944, she notes (I fancy, with regret) that the Anglican clergyman cannot, like a Roman priest, insist that at least one of the names given to a child shall be really Christian—taken, that is, from the Church calendar. Edward Lyford, she reminds us—'a pious young man', and an early worker on the interpretation of Christian names—wished 'that we should use such names as become Christians . . . Scripture names suitable to our estates and conditions'. The same wish, I should guess, inspired Mr. Keble's parishioner, Charlotte

[1] *The Oxford Dictionary of English Christian Names*, compiled by E. G. Withycombe, 1945.

M. Yonge, when she put together her *History of English Christian Names*. The Church, says Miss Withycombe, 'recognizes only the name given in baptism'; and she seems not quite certain whether we are entitled to any other names at all, even surnames. The House of Lords, she admits, has given judgement in a different sense. But 'George R. I.' is still good enough for the king; and the bishop of a diocese signs only his baptismal name. Yet how un-Christian some of these baptismal names are! Think of *Cosmo Gordon*.

Down to the end of the twelfth century the English names that were commonest were all un-Christian—*William*, *Robert*, *Ralph*, *Richard*. The first Christian name to assert itself was *John*. But in 1300 one Englishman in every seven was called *William*; not more than one in fifty bore the name *John*. *Matthew*, *Mark*, and *Luke* blessed nobody's cradle. *Thomas* came in with Thomas à Becket. After *John* and *William* it has been the most popular of all *praenomina*. Almost as popular has been *Henry*, or rather *Harry*—for until the seventeenth century *Harry* was the correct English form, appearing on the privy seals of six kings. The Reformation favoured the use of scriptural names. But it brought into disgrace and disuse the names of nonscriptural saints. The holy names of the Bible did not suffice for the large families of the Puritans. They fell back, sometimes on such unholy names as *Cain* and *Sapphira*, sometimes on 'improving' names of their own invention—as when Thomas Heley christened his four children *Much-Mercye*, *Increased*, *Sine-denie*, and *Fear-not*. For foundlings they found such names as *Misericordia-adulterina* and *Flee-fornication*.

Within living memory there were three brothers in Devonshire, decent fellows, but of Puritan stock, who carried the names *Shadrach*, *Meshach*, and *Abednego*. The Tottenham film-fans, with their *Garys* and *Shirleys*, seem in comparison amiable.

Books on Christian names are numerous. 'It must, however, be stated frankly', says Miss Withycombe, 'that they are for the most part almost valueless.' Her own book is, surely, good value. She acknowledges a debt to Bardsley's book on surnames; and she has used Förstemann's *Altdeutsches Namenbuch*. But her book is her own. She has gone for her material to documents; and it is the first book of the kind in which full use is made of the relevant historical records. For 'philological flights of fancy' she has no use. But it is a miracle how entertaining she manages to be. It is the only dictionary that I have ever read from cover to cover. I did it all between 11 p.m. and 2 a.m. on Christmas night; and I have never been better entertained. Now first I learned why half the *Margarets* in the world are called *Peggy* (via *Meggy*—cf. *Polly* and *Molly*); why *Jack* is the short for *John*, and has nothing to do with *Jacobus*; that *Dodo* stands for *Dorothy*, and has no connexion, as I had supposed, with the *Dodo* of the Bible; that *Camilla* is found as a girl's name in 1205, but not again until Miss Burney; that Shakespeare's *Imogen* is a mere misprint for *Innogen*; that *Elizabeth* is another form of *Isabel*; that *Oriel* is an Old German name, but that most of the girls christened *Oriel* of recent times are probably so called out of compliment to Oriel College; and much else of a like kind, good learning and good fun everywhere commingled.

Now and again I lifted my eyebrows in sceptical surprise. Miss Withycombe, I feel, should know better than to tell me that Erasmus's 'real name was Gerhard, which he erroneously supposed to mean "all heart", and translated into L. as *Desiderius* and into Gr. as *Erasmus*'. Erasmus was christened, like several of his contemporaries and one of his friends, after the martyr of the Diocletian persecution. Miss Withycombe's Greek scholarship is, I conjecture, less good than her English. Otherwise she would not give *Δημοσθένου* as the genitive of *Δημοσθένης*, nor say that *Θεόκλεια* was the feminine of *Θεόκλες*, nor call St. Paul's 'fellow-worker' *Φιλήμον*. I should have thought, again, that the name *Eubule* (borne by a distinguished living colonial governor) was derived rather from *εὔβουλος* than from *εὐβουλεύς*. But it is a shame to pick faults in so good a book.

THRILLERS

THE older I grow, the more inclined am I to ask of a book no more than that it should be readable. But so much I do ask. Already I am miserably old, I have a date with the world to come, and I cannot waste time reading unreadable books. If a book is, as books now tend to be, unprintable, that is not my affair; it is a matter for the Watch and Ward Committee. But if it is unreadable it touches me nearly. When I was young I used to like books that sent me to sleep. Now I like books that keep me awake; and above all books that keep me awake at night. I have reached a point when to see a 'thriller' is, I will not say to buy it, but to borrow it.

I like all thrillers, and I should have liked this paper to be about all classes of them. I like *Dracula* and I like *Drummond*; though I wonder why both of them make such good books and such indifferent plays. I like almost any book where either a house is haunted or a man hunted. But best of all I like books that deal with crime and detection. These give me my best thrills. These are for me thrillers *par excellence*: and it is these that my paper is going to be about, its wider title notwithstanding.

A few months ago I should have said that I had a better title to write about detective fiction than anyone else in the world—nobody in the world, I supposed, had both read so much of it and remembered so little. But I owe a grudge to Harvard; for I am easily beaten, I find, by both Professor

Lowes and Professor Kittredge. Perhaps I am still the best amateur of my subject—these two I feel to have forfeited their amateur status and to be living in a kind of open professionalism. Even so, in one particular I claim to be superior to them, and to bring to my subject better educated perceptions. With the criminal classes I have no more than a nodding acquaintance—though I have taught Latin verse to a man that was hanged. With detectives, real live detectives, I happen to have a quite intimate acquaintance. For a considerable period during the war I had under my charge six detectives from Scotland Yard, to say nothing of a spy from God knows where. Every Wednesday six detectives, complete with bowler hats, made secret reports to me upon conditions in certain scheduled areas. They had no imagination. What they said was so; and it was backed by countenances in which beer and benignity shone in about equal proportions. But I got to know all about detectives—to this day I can spot a detective anywhere in the streets of London. I have sometimes thought that it would be more useful to be friends with mere policemen. But I was really fond of my detectives—perhaps because I always felt that I was cleverer than they were. I was fond of the spy, too—I think I liked the spy best of all. Indeed, I made a kind of pet of him. He was called Archie; I was one of a few people who called him by his Christian name, and I am not sure that I ever knew his surname. He had more than one. I said that he came from God knows where; but at some time he had been in prison, and I daresay he is there now. There was a plot, you may remember, to murder Mr. Lloyd George by putting a poisoned nail in his boot. Archie was the principal witness for the Crown. But in the course of the trial it leaked out that not so many years back Archie had served three years for blackmail. It was impossible to put him in the witness-box. There was trouble over that: it was Archie's way to get everybody into trouble. But if ever I write a book 'Nice Men I have known', Archie will be in it.

Nothing is more interesting to me than to observe the classes of person to whom the detective novel makes its most special appeal. The great consumers of detective fiction are drawn, I find, from one or other of four fairly wide classes. First, cooks: female cooks. It may be their proverbial addiction to policemen; or it may be that the general fat comfortableness of their profession induces a reaction in favour of the life of imaginative action. Secondly, dons: professors and fellows of colleges. I have furnished two examples from Harvard, but I expect there are 200, if I knew it. I think it not a little remarkable that two of the best English writers of detective novels—G. D. H. Cole and R. A. Knox—should have been fellows of Oxford colleges. Cole, it is true, was a socialist, and Knox a Roman Catholic priest, the son, however, of an Anglican bishop of the old 'To-hell-with-the-Pope' school. These things might well turn a man's mind to murder. But I am not sure that it is not with us dons as with female cooks—we react against the general fat comfortableness of our lives; and also, what hardly happens with cooks, we react against an ever-present highbrowism. Perhaps the best collection of detective stories that exists is contained in a volume of the World's Classics, compiled and prefaced by the late Murray

Wrong, who was Vice-President of an Oxford college. Thirdly, there are the great statesmen. When I was a boy everybody read Gaboriau; and we might do worse than begin on him again. His detective stories were on every bookstall, with a distinctive red wrapper which I still recall well. Each wrapper was superscribed in large capitals 'The favourite reading of Prince Bismarck'. I can vouch for it again that one of the most distinguished English statesmen—which means that he was on my side of politics—read all the detective fiction that he could lay hands on—all of it that was printed (as much of it is) in Braille. I cannot think a statesman's life a comfortable one, or that he lives compassed by highbrowism. I would rather explain the addiction of this class to detective stories out of the interest they have in social stability and the forces of order; out of that, or else out of some mere cynicism or scepticism. And lastly, there are the surgeons and physicians and men of science. The names of Conan Doyle and Austin Freeman will occur to everyone. I do not think that either of those writers is much interested in the conception of crime as disease; nor will it naturally occur to a doctor to think of disease as a crime—obviously it is, for the doctor, a positive merit in a man to have something the matter with him. But habituation to corpses and a near familiarity with the various means of death naturally bring the doctor to reflect upon a good many of the subjects which supply the material of the detective novel. It has necessarily occurred to Austin Freeman, a scientist, that the worst difficulty that confronts a murderer is, what to do with the body? There *is* only one solution of it; and it was left to Freeman to discover it. The thing to do with the body is to give it to the British Museum. First, it is true, you have to treat it with formaldehyde; and for this purpose you require a bathroom and a garden-syringe. But with this not very elaborate equipment you can make of it, in a short space, a perfectly good mummy. You can take it round in a taxi-cab to the Department of Egyptology (an unsuspecting policeman will show you the way), and there you and the body will both be received with open arms.

Besides reflecting on how to get rid of dead bodies, Austin Freeman has given his attention to the subject of getting rid of live ones. It is often convenient to disappear, and the most satisfactory way of doing it, the most convincing to the police, is to get buried. This is quite easily done, and without personal inconvenience. You need neither die nor sham dead. Expert in medical science, Austin Freeman knows that Smith dead and Smith living are much less like than you and I would expect. Smith dead is in fact rather like Jones dead. If you put Jones on Smith's bed in Smith's clothes, and fetch the woman who makes Smith's bed, telling her on the way upstairs that Smith has had the misfortune to die in the night, she will without hesitation identify the dead body of Jones as that of Smith. She expected to see Smith, and Jones is about Smith's size, and has not got a beard either. Smith, accordingly, is safely certified as dead; and if a month later someone smuggles the Crown Jewels out of the Tower, it will not occur to the most astute detective that they were smuggled out by Smith.

However, a man cannot keep on being buried indefinitely, and there is presumably also a limit to the number of dead bodies which the British Museum will accept even from a well-accredited contributor. Accordingly, in most detective stories there is a perfectly obvious corpse and a not perfectly obvious murderer. Anything less than a corpse, let me say here and at once, creates in me a moral dissatisfaction. My self-esteem demands a corpse: I do not want to be called in to investigate a petty larceny. Even so grand a larceny as is involved in lifting the Crown Jewels falls short of the grandeur I seek. Wilkie Collins's *Moonstone* is, no doubt, a good detective story; stealing a moonstone is sufficiently like stealing the moon to make it interesting. But in general the dignity of detective fiction, and the voice of nature, cry out for a murder.

Immediately there arise a number of interesting questions of art, most of which I will not argue, but will be content simply to indicate the direction of my own taste. Aristotle praises Homer on the ground that he gets going quickly. 'Forthwith', he says, 'he brings on a man doing something.' I like a detective novel that gets going without palaver. I do not want to wait till Chapter Two for the crime. The proper place for a pistol-shot is the first paragraph. In respect of the more feminine crimes, smothering and strangling, I prefer that the deed should be done before the book opens. When it comes to *Who did it?*, let it be said plainly that there are certain persons who never ought to have done it; and it is a crime of fiction to saddle it on them.

First, the detective ought never to have done the crime. On the strength of my acquaintance with real live detectives I have no hesitation in ruling out at once from the first rank of detective fiction the novel in which the detective is the criminal. A detective is as little able to commit a crime in real life as he is, in fiction, able to detect one; he has neither the will nor the wit; and it is a bad fiction to give them to him. It is mostly the French, I think, who use this form of plot. It is used by Gaston Leroux. But it is a form of cheating; and besides being morally unsatisfactory, it can never, for anyone who has kept live detectives, have plausibility.

Secondly, the hero ought not to commit the crime; but he does so in Gilbert's *Mystery of the Open Window*. Still less, thirdly, ought the heroine to commit the crime; but the age of chivalry is dead, and she does so in Fielding's *Net Round Joan Ingleby*. A still worse outrage is it to art and to the moral sense when, fourthly, the author of the book himself commits the crime. At least such an outrage ought not to be allowed twice. It was first perpetrated by Agatha Christie in her *Murder of Roger Ackroyd*, where I am half-inclined to condone it, so well is the impudence of it carried. But I have met it since—for example, in Gregg's *Body in the Safe*—and resented it.

All these extravagances debauch the conscience of both the author and the reader. In general, the author, I am disposed to say, should play fair with his reader, but not too fair. While he ought not to be himself the criminal, he is necessarily an accomplice *ex post facto*. He knows; but we cannot expect him to let on. He is entitled to have us guessing. The novel where, as in some of Freeman's novels, or the play where, as in A. A. Milne's *Fourth Wall*, you are told from the beginning who did it, is never satisfactory as a story—it may offer us other satisfactions. About the novel where the crime is done by the obvious person, the person to whom all the clues point, I do not quite know what to say. The trouble about it is that more modern types have spoilt it for us. We are so used to the nuisance of novels in which the hero and the detective and the author and so on commit the crime that, in the straight story where the obvious person does it, we suspect everybody else.

Nor can we, I think, say outright that the story should be the kind of story that would give the real detective a chance. The real detective knows that heroes and heroines and authors do not commit crimes—he simply writes them off. But he knows that people generally do not commit crimes, at least not murders. Ladies and gentlemen and peers and peeresses—and the protagonists of the ideal detective story must be drawn from these classes—these classes commit adultery and take the name of God in vain and lie infinitely and sometimes commit small larcenies, but they almost never do murder. From the point of view of the real detective almost nobody in the book is capable of committing the crime. So much so that the real detective will be in some danger of dealing with the matter after the fashion of J. S. Fletcher, in one of whose books—I think *The Mazaroff Murders*—the deed is done by someone who does not appear in the book at all, or who only arrives in the last pages of it in time to be hanged.

For myself, I like best the novel in which you suspect everybody—save those persons for whom fair play demands, as I have said, that they should be above suspicion. As well as any recent novel I like, for this reason, Mr. and

Mrs. Cole's *Bletchington House Tangle.* Cole, besides being a fellow of an Oxford college, was a distinguished economic historian. You cannot suspect him and Mrs. Cole; and you cannot suspect the hero or the heroine, for the book has neither. But you do suspect everybody else. In fact, it is practically certain of each person in turn that he has done it. It has really been done by the most unlikely person of all, a peer of the realm. You and I would not suspect him. But you and I are not socialists—Mr. and Mrs. Cole were. But they wanted nobody's blood; rather weakly, to my mind, they let their criminal go free. Personally, I like somebody to be hanged. But if you do not insist on that, read the book.

So much detective fiction has been written of late in which the plot is conducted to a perverse and paradoxical conclusion that I marvel (I will here say in parenthesis) that no one has yet written a novel in which the wrong man is hanged. In the last chapter, the man who did it should, after dinner, over the curaçaos, take into his complete confidence the detective who failed to detect him. It will be to the obvious interest of either party to hush up a bad miscarriage of justice. But I am moved here, in another parenthesis, to utter a caveat to the tiro in detective fiction. The strongest temptation that can assail the tiro is the temptation to burlesque his art. Ronald Knox was somewhat a sinner in this respect; he was a Roman Catholic priest, and could not bring himself to be completely serious. Edgar Wallace also sinned once—in *The Brigand.* With the great body of consumers this will not go down. They are a serious crowd, with that pale bloodthirsty seriousness on which light irony is lost. For them any hint of burlesque is the sin that hath no forgiveness.

The Bletchington House Tangle succeeds in being a novel of many suspects for a reason which, I think, throws light on the most real problem that detective fiction offers. The plot of it is good because the characters are only lightly sketched. The most usual fault of detective stories is a clash between character and action. In a well-constructed work of fiction, whether it be novel or drama, character and action hang together; a man does what he is, and he is what he does. But the soul of a detective novel is suspicion; and you cannot suspect a man if you know him too well. If his character lies plain, no assault of circumstance, however ingeniously arranged, is going to damage or compromise him. In a good detective novel the characters should be so far well drawn that you do not know them too well. In a bad detective story what commonly happens is that they are not *well* drawn, but *sharply* drawn; with one of two consequences: either you know that a given person *cannot* have done it, and he has not, or he *has* done it and ought not to have done it. In the one case you are bored, and in the other you are morally affronted. It is the difficulty of reconciling character and action that makes really good detective stories rare. They are rare. On the other hand, moderately good ones are astonishingly plentiful. I am glad always to have a moderately good one; and the recipe for it, I have no doubt, is that the writer should concentrate on plot and not break his heart over characterization. The characters that he need not be afraid of are those who ought always, I have urged, to stand outside suspicion: above all the detective and the hero and heroine. These characters may safely be elaborated without any fear of giving things away.

Consistent with this is the fact that the best detective novels plainly *are* those in which the character of the detective is developed with some elaboration. On the whole, the good detective novel is the one which has a good detective in it; a detective who, besides detecting, has character: Lecoq, Sherlock Holmes, Dr. Thorndyke, Hanod, Superintendent Wilson, Philo Vance. Let me confess that I like my detective to have a few human weaknesses. I like Sherlock Holmes the better for his addiction to cocaine. ' "For me now", says Dr. Watson, "what remains?" "For me", says Holmes, "the cocaine bottle." ' This weakness in Holmes seems to explain, incidentally, what is otherwise inexplicable—how he managed to tolerate Dr. Watson. Obviously, the doctor was the source of the drug. It is an ugly reflection; but it makes things human.

Personally, I do not like women detectives, even titled ones like Lady Molly of Scotland Yard. I hate women with fingers of whipcord and wrists like steel. I hate that a straight criminality should be beaten by coquetry; and again I hate the indecorums in which the female detective necessarily becomes involved. Nor can I persuade myself that a detective story ought to have a love-interest. Again, I cannot bear seeing my detective cry. In general, women seem to me, for what reason I know not, to make good spies and bad detectives. Perhaps they are better at ferreting things out than at thinking them out.

But I do not want, even so, to have my detective fiction too intellectual. The good detective should be kept, I feel, both thinking and doing. Of Edgar Wallace it is the grand merit that something happens in every chapter. *The Green Archer* deserves all its popularity, just for the manner in which it keeps going. In truth, I like best, not merely those detective stories which subordinate character to action, but those in which thought also is, on the whole, secondary. I hardly dare say so, but I do not even very much mind if the solution of my mystery is a little loose and inferior, provided I get a full measure of excitement. I like episode, and I do not much fret for unity in the structure of my story. After all, this is not the Greek drama; it is a way of keeping oneself awake and of surviving a railway journey. A good many writers of detective novels keep the nose of the reader, I feel, too much on the grindstone. I hate maps and diagrams and complicated time-table calculations. I hate Colonel Gore's *deductions*—though I like much else about him; they are too near to real thinking. I am sometimes a little bored, again, with Dr. Thorndyke's science; but here, not because I am made to think, but because I do not possess the material for doing so. Too many of Austin Freeman's plots turn on some piece of scientific knowledge which the reader does not possess. Dr. Thorndyke can never be such good fun as Holmes; because while nobody knows that you can make a mummy by injecting formaldehyde into a corpse everybody knows that, if you pawn your watch, the pawnbroker makes a little scratch upon it. Everybody, again, knows that a man who winds his watch with a key when he is not quite sober makes a big scratch upon it. It was thus that Holmes inferred that Dr. Watson's brother had once been poor and taken to drink. This was

Watson's dark secret; only Holmes knew it; and Watson bought his silence with cocaine.

Are detective stories good for us—in all the present plethora of them? I ask the question; but it is a detestable question, and I have scarce the patience to try and answer it. The truth is that nearly all books are good for us; they are better for us than men and women. Exciting books are especially good for us, because nothing is so bad for us as to be dull. But above all, those books are good for us which make us morally better. Detective fiction has the advantage over all other kinds in that, in this kind only, virtue always triumphs. There are detective novels that do not always end in the vindication of the law. But they do vindicate morals—there is none I know in which the cause of morality is not, in the long run, vindicated. In the detective novel the reader is sustained throughout by a sure and certain expectation of the triumph of the moral order.

But what, I shall be asked, what about a book like *Raffles*? Do you like a book of which the hero ought to be in prison? At least I prefer it, I shall answer, to a book of which the author ought to be in prison.

Perhaps it is the glory of detective novels, not to be good, but to be *good enough*. There is no pretence about them; they are as honest as literary work can be. They carry no nonsense of high art. They find a man bored, and they keep him amused. They see him in his perpetual peril of becoming a prig, and they snatch him from it into good sense and good temper. And last, for we are all ailing flesh, they often find a man sick, and stay with him till he is well again. I think this is their kindliest office.

'FAIR HARVARD'

IN the course of a life already too long, I have paid three visits to the United States. I can claim, I should suppose, to be the only Englishman who has spent eighteen months in America without knowing all about it—I have never even written a book about it. And I should not be writing this paper for the Bodley Club if I had not had my wrist twisted by your secretary.

I do not know all about America; and I do not know all about Harvard. Everything I know about either I like—excepting always their food and their drink. The food is not so bad as German or Dutch food; nor the drink so bad as no drink at all. But both are bad; and I often beg Englishmen, whenever they feel disposed to criticize Americans, to remember that most of the faults of the American character proceed, almost certainly, from the character of American food.

The title of my paper, the phrase 'fair Harvard', comes from one of the Harvard drinking songs; and to a man who has had plenty to drink, and is born good-natured, it may pass as a tolerable description of the external aspect of the place. Some of the Harvard buildings are as good as could be—those, namely, which are built in the Georgian—or, as they call it, 'colonial'—style. The next best are those which imitate these—most of them built in the present century. But one or two of the halls are as bad as Butterfield[1]—and

[1] See 'Max and Merton College', above.

a little like him; and the general grouping of the buildings is loose and unsatisfactory. The heart of the university is the yard, containing the older halls and the principal university offices.

Harvard is distinguished from all other American universities by having a yard, instead of a *campus*. The yard is a roughly rectangular space, equal perhaps in area to the Christ Church Meadow, and enclosed by a wall, or the remains of one. Once there was a perfectly good wall; but today it is not much more than a collection of Memorial Gates. Each gate commemorates, usually in Latin, some great deed, or great man, of American history, or some eminent American virtue: there is a gate labelled, as you might expect, *Veritas*. I never counted the gates; but if Egyptian Thebes had a hundred, Harvard will make not a bad second to Egyptian Thebes.

The yard, then, is enclosed by gates embroidered with the remains of a wall. But even so, it is not shut in. Day and night the gates of Harvard stand open, a symbol at once of the accessibility of learning and of the liberty-loving temper of the American people. The safety of Harvard depends, like that of the ideal Greek city, not upon its walls, but upon its men, who are, in this case, the yard-cops. A yard-cop is a college policeman. He looks like a professor; and the professors, there as here, look like men wanted by the police. The yard-cop exists to cop the bootlegger; and in fact earns his living by not doing so. In marked contrast with the street-cop he enjoys a considerable popularity with the students. When an undergraduate club holds a dinner, outside the club lurks a yard-cop, to warn the diners of any lurking street-cop. No street-cop may venture within the walls or gates of Harvard. But they get their own back outside. They are thought not to fight fair. They carry guns; and I have myself witnessed a fight in the street between three heavily armoured street-cops and a naked undergraduate.

This leads me to say something about the clothes of the Harvard undergraduate. This particular man was not naked when the fight began. He was wearing 'trunks'—a garment considered by the police to be inadequate, and which in any case fell from him in the fray. There is nothing the matter with 'trunks', except the absurd name. Over the length and breadth of America pants are trunks, trousers are pants, a gym-shirt is a vest; shoes are called boots, a bowler-hat is a Derby, braces are called suspenders, suspenders garters. My very first day in Harvard I disgraced myself before a girl. I wanted, and I asked for, a pair of suspenders. She said, 'I expect you mean garters'; and I said, 'No, they are for myself.' She brought me braces; and I said, 'No, I want suspenders.' Before I got what I wanted, a small crowd had collected to hear me explaining that what was slipping down was not my trousers, but my socks.

The Harvard student wears all the garments I have mentioned. Custom prescribes that he shall be well dressed, except at the extremities. His boots must be old, and he must not have them cleaned, or, as they call it, shined. His hat must be so old as to be past shining. He must wear a suit, and not flannel trousers. If the temperature is below seventy degrees, he must wear an overcoat; if he is somebody, it must be a fur coat. A fur coat costs, say, eighty pounds. But the parent of a Harvard 'boy' (they are all 'boys', or call themselves so) will make any sacrifice rather than that his son should want a fur coat. Though he wraps himself up like an invalid, I may say here, the Harvard student is essentially robust—they are perhaps the most manly race in the world. Nothing struck me so much, coming home, as how feminine, in comparison, our young men looked—and how masculine all our young women.

Twenty-four per cent., it is calculated, of American students earn their living, or a part of it, while they are going through college. Many of them do pretty rough work, and get a knowledge of men and a perception of life much greater than that which an English undergraduate has. Whether the gain in robustness compensates for the loss of learning entailed may be questioned—much depends on what you conceive education to mean. I fancy that the poor student in America often overworks himself physically and mentally. In America, be it remembered, a university degree is worth working for; it helps a man in life. To have been at Harvard opens doors in business; to have been at Oxford shuts them. Partly on this account the average Harvard undergraduate seems to me a great deal more industrious than the average Oxford undergraduate. He really wants to get through his examinations. The Harvard dons also work much harder than our dons. Their lectures are reported on annually in the *Harvard Crimson*, an undergraduate daily paper. The reports are written by undergraduates; they are usually fresh and forcible; and there are professors who look forward to their annual reports very much as schoolboys look forward to their terminal reports. As a result there is, I fancy, a too general disposition to believe that to every question in literature, philosophy, or religion, there is a right and a wrong answer. Here we are content with good and bad answers; employing a method which I cannot but think a better instrument for the discovery of truth. I may say here, without offence, that I never quite got the hang of Harvard—that I was bad in discussions with students, just because of what I say. When I opened my heart in discussion, somebody was sure to write it down, supposing it to be a right answer, when it was merely a good one—a good answer to a question that ought never to have been asked. I had a weekly at-home day for such discussions. But the truth of it was that nobody was really at home, I least of all. Nobody ever contradicted me—and if I contradicted myself nobody noticed it.

The Harvard student is, I think, not easy to know. What is called the 'Harvard indifference' has passed into a proverb—somewhat like the 'Oxford manner'. The 'Oxford manner' is found in its perfection, of course, in Cambridge; and the 'Harvard indifference' belongs, I suspect, exclusively to Princeton and Yale. The Harvard undergraduate is so far not indifferent that I should suppose him to be more shy and self-conscious than any creature in the world short of an Englishman. Half his thinking is thinking what you are thinking about him. The other half consists in thinking that you were necessarily educated at Eton, where you shined the boots of a nobleman, who beat you in a degrading fashion, so that you lost all taste for human freedom.

To freedom the Harvard student attaches very great importance. The gates of Harvard, I have said, stand always open. The Harvard student has not got to be in at twelve—he has not got to be in at all, unless he wishes. He may go to bed when, or where, he likes, or not at all; he can get up when he likes. He marvels at the restrictions to which the Oxford undergraduate submits so tamely—gates, roll-calls, proctors, and the like. On the other hand, the Harvard student, at any rate in his first year, submits without murmur to a regulation which we should regard as slavish to a degree—compulsory games. He submits without a murmur, again, to compulsory medical examination; this periodical vetting is part of an enforced first-year course in hygiene. A good many students combine a course in hygiene with a course in the history of religion. If the American mind sometimes seems to want *mystery*, it is because, with many of them, morality has been reduced to hygiene and religion to an antiquarian study. The Harvard student, again, does not feel his liberty seriously curtailed if he is made to share, not only a sitting-room, but a bedroom with one or more men whom he has never seen before. The truth is, of course, that human beings, either side of the water, care much less for freedom than they suppose; what they do care for is what they are used to.

From this point of view, I found myself in Harvard at an interesting time. The university had just committed itself to the so-called 'House Plan'; an experiment destined—so some persons suppose—to transform completely the

American conception of university life. Four million dollars were to be expended in building four Houses, each holding about 250 students, each as like an Oxford college as an American is like an Englishman. I did not give the money myself; but I was sometimes treated as though I had. Every Oxford man was suspect. He was part of a plot to Oxfordize Harvard. The old Harvard liberty was threatened. Each of the new Houses, or colleges, was to have a master. If you lived in a House with a master, you were a slave. There was to be a High Table: this was an especial offence—the Harvard undergraduate could not see why the dons should not eat with the undergraduates; the reason why is, of course, that the undergraduates would be bored stiff. Every man was to have a sitting-room and bedroom to himself. This was called 'solitary confinement'. So many meals per week in hall were to be compulsory. This, again, was an attack on elementary liberty. It was an end of 'eating around'. 'Eating around' is the most characteristic feature of Harvard life. Meals in college are, or were, unknown. A man ate where he would, and what food he would—mostly, I have hinted, food that nobody else would. To the rattle and roar of the cheap cafeteria he had an attachment almost bloodthirsty. Now, like an Oxford undergraduate, he was to dress every night for dinner, and be waited on, Oxford-fashion, by a powdered lackey in yellow-plush livery. There was to be grace before dinner; and each House was to be a hotter hotbed of snobbery than the others.

Everybody resolved that he would not put his name down for any one of the new Houses. The first two are built; they were built, *more Americano*, in about two days. For each of them the applicants were double in number what the House could hold. The evil which had been most feared was that which, when it came, nobody minded—social snobbishness. Everybody had made up his mind that no House should be anything but a true cross-section of Harvard life—it should represent all classes. I had a letter the other day from a student at one of the new Houses. 'You will remember', he wrote, 'the true-cross-section stunt; and will find an interesting comment on it in the fact that, except for myself and another boy from Georgia, every boy in the House comes from Groton or St. Mark's or St. Paul's or St. George's' (i.e. Eton, Harrow, Winchester, Charterhouse—only that these are cheap schools, in comparison).

I hit here an evil which I have no wish to exaggerate. But if I were asked wherein Harvard is least like Oxford, I should feel obliged to say that it is in the sharpness of the social distinctions that it makes, and in the grounds on which those distinctions are based. The social aristocracy of Harvard consists of the men from the private schools. They are a small minority; but they dominate. A man may be a nice man, *and* he may be a good athlete; but unless he has been to a private school it will not help him in the day of social judgement. I had friends in the Harvard football team who came from public schools. The men from the private schools who played in the same team with them did not speak to them in the streets.

In comparison with that, we are, I think, democratic. Whether we should be quite so democratic if we were situated as Harvard is, I am not so sure. The fact is that in Oxford we are marvellously protected from women. Women are the fountain-head of social distinctions. Here, in Oxford, we are democratic. But I wonder whether, in our homes, we are not mostly unashamed snobs. Harvard is situated on the confines of two large and wealthy cities, each with a fashionable life of its own. The Harvard undergraduate takes his social position among his fellows very largely according to the houses in Boston and Cambridge which accept him. It is the women who work this havoc. The social life of the Harvard student is quite surprisingly different from the social life of an Oxford undergraduate. In the life of the private-school man and the public-school man women play an infinitely greater part. Owing to the wealth of the country, men marry early; and the thought of getting married is constantly present to the minds of most of the students. Many of their amusements and pleasures centre, not on the common social life, but on a social life in which women share. This is partly due to the proximity of two fashionable towns, but partly also to the defects—or what seem to an Englishman the defects—of the college system as it has existed till the other day. The student halls are not colleges, the new Houses are not (I believe) going to be colleges. They are what they are called: 'dormitories'. A man's room, or set of rooms, is in no sense at all the pivot of his social life. The high cost of service makes meals in rooms, and entertaining in rooms, prohibitive. The function of rooms is fulfilled when you sleep and work in them. Hospitalities are extra-mural; and companionship—the breaking of bread together—a public business.

The Harvard man's life is, indeed, or seemed to me to be, too much lived in public. As a rule he has a room-mate. He may have two. Three men may very likely share, not only one sitting-room, but one bedroom. Never is a man alone; but works, sleeps, eats, plays in public. From the highest of all arts—that of possessing his soul—he remains impossibly excluded.

I say that, and I have made one or two other criticisms, at my proper peril. It is not likely, I mean, that, thrown for nine months among customs and institutions both strangely like and strangely unlike our own, I should not be at sea about a hundred vital matters. I began by saying that I did not know all about Harvard. And apart from any other difficulties that I might have, it is a place of youth; and I should be sorry to suppose that, carrying those years I do, I had any chance of penetrating to the things that count. A good many dons from English colleges go there nowadays; I wish more young men went. The language is not easy to learn; but the people are extraordinarily well worth knowing. If there are any Americans among my audience, I hope they will forgive me for saying that I was miserable at the idea of going there; for at least I was miserable over coming away. I still find it hard to keep going without seeing an occasional American. My colleagues tell me that I have developed a sort of drug-habit, and that I cannot get along without a daily American . . . And I *do* find it tonic. Oxford has something about it a little relaxing. Anyone of us, I feel, would be the better for a year in Harvard. I hated the food; but I did love the folk.

DOGS

I HAVE had many dogs. But the last of them has always been the best. At the moment, I have one dog only. A Sealyham of distinguished lineage, he is as beautiful as it is permitted to a Sealyham to be. In fact he raises for me, every day, the whole problem of beauty. To look upon him is to dismiss summarily the Greek and easy notion that the primary characters of the beautiful are symmetry and proportion. It is difficult, indeed, looking at him, not to allow ethical considerations to obtrude themselves on aesthetic theory. His countenance expresses, before all else, benignity, his eyes have moral depth. A pacifist could not look more disarming, a bishop or a butler more decorous. But it is pure take-in. Whatever lives and moves, he chevies, and if he does not kill all that he catches, it is not his fault. He has been too long with me, even so, to have any faults. For I cannot account it a fault that he looks beautiful without meaning it.

Hardly had I written these few lines about this faultless creature than war and age and deafness and blindness came to him in swift succession, making life unintelligible to him. If it had been intelligible, I do not know that he would have been happier. In an untranquil world, he enjoyed tranquillity. That song the sirens sang nightly meant nothing to him. He continued to think men better than they were. With a good conscience, subject to no orders—since he heard none—he went where he would, or could, and did what he liked, the defect of sight and hearing quickening, it may be, curiosity. He went where he would, and he did what he liked, however feebly. Until, one winter morning, going where he would, but not knowing where, he walked, in the uncertain dawn, into one of those static-water-ponds with which the war studded our gardens; and the half-frozen waters closed over the loveliest of old heads that ever wanted brains—for he had no cleverness. I have had many dogs. At my feet, as I write, lies yet another Sealyham. I have had many dogs, and, until now, the last has always been the best. Now, the last but one must always be the best and dearest to me. The earth is over him; but the earth of his own garden. A tall sycamore shadows his grave. In a hollow bough of it nests, unmolested now, a family of squirrels, whom, while he lived, he persecuted with infinite frustrate ardour. That old feud those old foes can afford to forget.

When and where men first came to love dogs, I have no idea. In the literatures with which I am most familiar, those of antiquity, the dog comes off poorly. With the Jews—as with the Eastern peoples generally—he is everywhere a despised creature. 'Is thy servant a dog?'—'grin like a dog and run about through the city'—that is the kind of thing you get about the dog in the Bible. As for the Greeks, we have all, I fancy, been bamboozled by Homer, or by reading Homer with insufficient attention. Nobody who has read either Homer or Pope is likely to forget the scene in which the dog Argus recognizes Ulysses. But it is easy to miss some of the implications of it. Argus is a hunting-dog, a κύων θηρευτής. That is the only kind of dog Homer recognizes. Except for the grand purpose of hunting, only decadents keep dogs. Ulysses had bred Argus a hunting-dog. But he had never hunted him. He had been called to the wars. In his absence, the young men about the place had, in fact, used Argus to hunt hares and goats and deer. When he was past that use, they had used him very much as the Jews used dogs, to do scavenging. Ulysses, when he came home, after twenty years of war-service,[1] found him busy with the dung-heaps and full of vermin. He does not know him. Is he a hunting-dog, he asks (the only good kind of dog), or a mere domestic dog, one of those despised dogs that the decadent rich keep for show?—

> Such dogs, and men, there are, mere things of state,
> And always cherished by their friends, the Great.

Pope's rendering is just clever eighteenth-century falsification. For not a word has Homer about the pampered *men*. Nor is it only here that Pope interpolates. The women, says Homer, do not bother about Argus. The women, says Pope,

> keep the generous creature bare,
> A sleek and idle race is all their care.

Homer's women may, like his decadent young men, keep handsome table-dogs to pet and pamper. But it is only Pope who says so.

Be all that as it may, for Ulysses the only dog is the hunting-dog; the domestic dog spells decadence. And that

[1] Aristotle (*H.A.* vi. 21) is a little uneasy over the age of Argus. But some people think, he says, that a dog *may* live to be twenty.

is, generally, I fancy, the Greek view. Why, else, except that they did not really like dogs, is the shameless man, or woman, called *κυνώπης, κυνῶπις*? Why is the Cynic so called, except for opprobrium? Why does Socrates swear only 'by the dog'? The *historian* of the dog, and of the chase, may read profitably Xenophon's *Cynegeticus*. But the lover of the dog will get little from it. The Jews never hunted—how should they? The Greeks hunted; for reasons that, today, we should think old-fashioned. Hunting and dogs, Xenophon tells us, were devised by the gods. They imparted their secret to Chiron, because he practised justice. People interested in hunting, Xenophon says, will find many benefits from it. It gives men good physical health, it improves their hearing and their eyesight, and, above all, it trains them for war. The dog makes possible the huntsman, the huntsman the soldier. And there the matter ends. Of the dog as 'the friend of man' Greek literature has little to say. What little there is must be sought in the Palatine Anthology—most of it dating from the Greek decadence. In Mackail's Selection from the Anthology the curious reader will find (in Greek and English) three delightful epitaphs on dogs. One of them, assigned to Simonides, commemorates a *hunting*-dog—Simonides was before the decadence; another, a watch-dog. The watch-dog was called Bull for his deep voice. 'Bull they called him, while yet he lived. But now the silent pathways of night possess the voice of him' —*φθέγμα σιωπηραὶ νυκτὸς ἔχουσιν ὁδοί*. With an epitaph ending on a line so languorous, so decadently beautiful, he is well enshrined.

The third of Mackail's three Epitaphs appeals to the

passer-by not to think it absurd and laughable that a dog should have a tomb and a graven verse. Who but a Jew or Greek or Roman could think it absurd? For the Romans, in respect of the dog, are no better than the Greeks. I think, indeed, that they are worse. The Latin is a dogless literature. I know of but two dogs that live in it; and they in a fashion not particularly distinguished. Martial's friend Publius had a dog called Issa. So beautiful and virtuous a creature was Issa that a double immortality was devised for her. She was painted by a perfect artist; and Martial made for the occasion an epigram perfect in its triviality. Who Publius was, I know not. But some decadent, surely; the piece comes late in time. Later still, and less perfect, is an epitaph preserved in the Latin anthology, commemorating a dog called Pearl. 'France bore me, the pearl of the rich sea gave me my name, a gay name apt to my beauty. . . . Though I was but a dog my dumb lips had an eloquence beyond what belonged to my kind.' Years ago, I saved 'Pearl' from oblivion in the anthology, making a place for her in the *Oxford Book of Latin Verse*. I say 'her'; betraying her sex. But I have to call her 'dog'; it is difficult to say why.

Publius' Issa had her portrait painted. The only portrait of a Latin dog that I know is that of the mosaic floor in Pompeii. He is a small aggressive dog, snarling visibly, held in by a chain or leash. Scrawled underneath are the familiar words 'Cave Canem'.

'Cave Canem', Englished 'Beware of the Dog', I recall from my boyhood as a not uncommon inscription on the gates of west-country farms. We must beware, therefore, what inferences we draw from the walls of Pompeii. Even so, the Romans, I believe, did not like dogs. Nor the Greeks either, nor the Jews, least of all the Jews. That the dog came into his own with Christianity and loving-kindness, I am not going to say. We began, I must think, we lovers of dogs, much as less loving races; we began with the dog as a thing useful—the dog of the chase, the sheep-dog, the watch-dog, the blind man's dog. I recall nothing from antiquity about the blind man's dog; nor, indeed, much about that grand disaster of the senses, blindness. It was something, it would seem, rather venerable than pitiful. Did anybody *pity* Homer, or Tiresias, or Phineus? And did any of these keep dogs? Or were they led altogether by the spirit? Milton never, that I know of, kept a dog. He kept daughters; and he would like to have kept wives. If anybody led him about, these did. Is there any other poet, I wonder, who never, whether in prose or poetry, mentions the dog, except only as a Jew might, with disrespect? I ought, perhaps, in saying that, to except what is said of the dog in one of the Latin *Prolusions*. The *Prolusions* take us back to Milton's undergraduate youth. I would like to think that, as an undergraduate, he kept a dog. But in truth, the praise which, in the seventh *Prolusion*, he bestows on the dog is not his own, but borrowed, confessedly, from Plutarch. The dog, we are told, is not ignorant of dialectic. If the dog comes to a place where three roads meet, he uses the disjunctive syllogism. The dog spoken of is, in fact, the hunting-dog. I think we can be sure that Milton hated hunting.

The blind man's dog we can leave out of account. He is

the poor man's dog; and, like poverty, has no business to exist. It is not often, I should suppose, that he possesses beauty. The hunting-dog, for Ulysses, is essentially beautiful. But not beautiful if he is not hunted. I am not sure that Ulysses recognizes any dogs that are not hunting-dogs. The table-dog whom he speaks of unkindly seems to be only the hunting-dog withdrawn from the fields to the dining-room. He does not deny the beauty of him; but he cannot bear that he should not be useful and used. That the watch-dog was esteemed for his beauty nothing, I think, indicates. 'Bull', the watch-dog of the Palatine anthology, owes his credit to his voice, the depth of his bay. The Pompeii watch-dog is rather specially unlovely. But he is there for his yap—bay he cannot, he is too small. The shepherd's dog, we may suspect, became domesticated early. In the shepherd's hut he has a natural place. But what except his beauty brought him into the parlours of the rich it would be hard to say. What dog, and of what kind, is the earliest domesticated dog in English literature I should not like to guess. The earliest that I know I find in the earliest of our poets whom I can be said to know, in any real sense. Chaucer's Prioress kept dogs. But of what species, except that they were small, we are not told:

> Of smale houndes hadde she, that she fedde
> With rosted flessh, or milk and wastel-breed.
> But soore she wepte if oon of hem were deed,
> Or if men smoot it with a yerde smerte;
> And al was conscience and tendre herte.

The 'tendre herte' of Madame Eglantine we may take for

granted. But she was certainly not 'al conscience'—as we understand conscience.[1] For by the rules of their order nuns were not allowed to keep dogs. Whether she took her dogs with her to Canterbury the context does not make plain. I think Chaucer brings in the dogs, not because they accompanied their mistress, but just because he was aware that nuns might not keep dogs. He likes her the better for disobeying. For he passes immediately to his Monk, who

> yaf nat of that text a pulled hen
> That saith that hunters ben nat hooly men. . . .
> Therefore he was a prikasour aright:
> Greyhondes he hadde as swift as fowel in flight;
> Of prikyng and of huntyng for the hare
> Was all his lust, for no cost wolde he spare.

These 'smale houndes' of the Prioress I take to be the first domesticated dogs in our poetry—and the poetry of dogs to begin with women. The monks hunted, and the nuns kept table-dogs—against religion—and Chaucer likes both classes the better for it. Homer, I fancy, would not have liked Madame Eglantine's table-dogs; he would have scented the beginnings of decadence. For it is likely, I think, that to women we owe the dog in the house, the dog that (utility apart) serves as companion and friend. Tolstoy says somewhere that all children prefer women to men—there is no exception, he alleges. The same is true, I fancy, of dogs. It is through women that they became a part of the house, and they know it—out of infinite time they remember it. I used to suppose that it was Voltaire who said:

[1] By 'conscience' Chaucer, no doubt, meant 'sensibility'.

'The more I see of men, the better I like dogs.' I had supposed it said cynically, and not much real kindness intended to the dog. But it was not Voltaire, I find. It was said by a woman. It was said by Madame Roland.

For most of us, the dog means the house-dog. To the average man he is the dog that matters; for the average man cannot afford to hunt and shoot. That, often enough, our 'smale houndes', and the greater ones, are sporting dogs, is only accident. Essentially, they exist, not to be used, but to be loved. It is absurd, feminine, decadent; and we make all sorts of excuses for ourselves. Very often we put it upon the children—the children must have a dog in the house. In truth, it is we who are the children. We put ourselves first, and the dog, some of us, before the children. I have known many men who disliked children, their own not excluded. But not many men dislike dogs; and those that do rarely confess to it. To suggest to an Englishman that he does not like dogs is a studied insult. The cat any man may dislike. If I do not much like cats, I have a reason for it. Of all God's creatures the cat is the most conceited. I say nothing of its cruelty; nothing of the cold malice of its mischief. A dog takes something because it wants it, because it cannot withstand temptation. The cat takes things, not because it wants them, but because it prefers wrong to right. The faults of the dog are few and involuntary. Most of the dogs that I have kept have had, in fact, no faults at all. Other people have complained of them, people who do not like dogs; and to that I have always a ready rejoinder, they do not like dogs. The truth is that the dog has become established in the house for sheer moral quality.

If he has not got all the virtues, he has the appearance of them. It is easy to say that he takes us in. But even if he does, does it matter? What matters is that we love him, ultimately, because we love moral quality.

I write fresh from reading Stevenson's essay on *The Character of Dogs*. The Scots—Sir Walter especially—are always good on dogs. But Stevenson seems to me to have got the character of the dog all wrong. 'The day of an intelligent small dog', he writes, 'is passed in the manufacture of and the laborious communication of falsehood; he lies with his tail, he lies with his eye, he lies with his protesting paw; and when he rattles his dish or scratches at the door his purpose is other than appears.' Not so have I known Skyes, nor Aberdeens, nor any species of dog. And not a syllable does Stevenson add in support of a statement which anybody who has ever kept a dog knows to be false and base, and not clever at that. Some apology he makes for the lying dog. For himself, the lying writer, there can be none. The dog, he says, caught in a lie, at once confesses and is patently penitent. He knows the difference between truth and falsehood—which cannot be said of all men; and he is sorry. When he barks or bites, and is rebuked or chastened for it, it is different. He is not sorry.

Here, and in other connexions, I marvel how little we any of us really know about dogs; though upon none of the lower creatures has so much affectionate study been lavished. The delight that dogs proverbially have in barking and biting is intelligible. But there is one behaviour of the fighting dog which has no explanation, or none that a thinking person can accept as plausible. I have had more than one fighting dog, and have known a good many others. But never one that fought *unaccompanied.* I can turn my dog loose any day in the Christ Church Meadows. He will meet half a hundred dogs, mixing with any of them harmlessly. But, accompanied (whether by his master or by a deputy, it matters not), accompanied, he attacks whatever dog he sees. I am told by people who know no better that he supposes himself to be protecting his master. As if he did not suppose his master to be all-powerful! Or I am told that he is 'showing off'. As though he did not know that I knew he could fight! My own opinion in the matter is not worth much; for, as I say, really, none of us know about dogs. My own opinion is that he fights when accompanied from a knowledge that, if things come to the worst, he will be pulled off alive. No dog worth the name ever lets go; and except they are separated by human intervention, a battle between dogs must end fatally for the one party or the other.

Nothing does my dog like as much as a walk. But what dog walks alone? Yet why should he never, alone, indulge his dearest pleasure? Here, too, does he play for safety? The garden, the adjoining meadow, the small lane at the head of the meadow—all these my dog frequents. But only because they are home ground, or because he supposes them to be home ground; he can get access to all of them without any opening of gates or clambering over defensive walls. But a ten-mile walk (he can do twenty) never enters his head, unless he can find a human companion. Yet for such a walk, properly companioned, he will, any day, leave his very dinner. It is no good saying, with Stevenson, that he is the mere 'satellite of man', betrayed into that position by his 'rage for consideration'. The same might be said of any one of us that cultivates friendship. The dog prefers human companionship to anything else in the world. For that miracle we love him; and when we think what some men are, it is a considerable miracle.

Coming back to my own dog, and to fighting: he was eighteen months old when he began it. Till then, he was gentle to the verge of timidity. He put off that character only when I took him, one summer, into the country. He put it off, not from meeting there other dogs, but from making his first acquaintance with horses, bullocks, wild deer. He began upon horses. There was a fieldful of them before his dining-room window. Curiosity—a rather timid curiosity, I think—took him there. All he asked was a scamper, in perfect friendliness. That these horses—to his diminutive stature mountains—should be afraid of him never entered his head. Nor, I suppose, were they. But as he scampered towards them, they scampered from him, irritated by, albeit despising, so small a creature. They showed their irritation by lashing out at him with their feet, ineffectively. To him, what mattered was that they scampered. They *fled*, ten to a dozen giants before an excited dwarf of a dog. Then it was that to this small creature it occurred, for the first time, that he was somebody. What should I think myself if lions and tigers habitually fled before me? I should make the fatal mistake of life, I should think myself somebody. Casting off fear, I should indulge all sorts of impertinences. He began with the horses. Next, he tried it, with the same results, on the bullocks. The deer were less frequent, and there was less fun to be had with them. But between them they changed a modest and timorous dog into a dog combative and self-confident beyond all reason. How should the tallest of dogs, thereafter, wait the onset of a creature before whom horses of I know not how many hands, and bullocks with demonstrable horns, had again and again fled ignominiously? If my dog fights other dogs, it is not because he is their enemy, but because he has been the victor of horses, bullocks, deer. He thinks he is somebody.

Why has no one made an anthology of the literature of dogs? Why is there no Oxford Book of Dogs? To anyone who will undertake it, I make a present of Issa and Pearl and Bull. Cerberus and Argus he will think of for himself. When he has done with them, he will know perhaps whether Cerberus had fifty heads or a hundred, or three only. When he comes to modern times, he will hardly miss Chaucer's Nun and Monk. I hope he will not, with Chaucer, be disposed to think the religion of hunting better than true religion. If he does, let him correct himself out of Boswell, who records a memorable utterance of Johnson about hunting: 'It is very strange', said Johnson, 'and very melancholy that the paucity of human pleasures should persuade us ever to call hunting one of them.' More pertinently, let him recall from Boswell, when he recalls the portrait of Issa made for the decadent Publius, that, if it did not seem decadent to Johnson, at least it seemed absurd and preposterous, that a man should wish to have his dog painted. For so, I think, we must interpret Johnson when he says, 'I would rather see the portrait of a dog I knew than all the allegorical painting that they can shew me in the world.' Johnson could see no good, or no pleasure that could be found, in hunting. That is not English, but I see sense in it, and morals. But alas! Dr. Johnson hated dogs. 'What could be more foolish', he asks, 'than the washing and combing of a dog; one's nature revolts at such an absurdity! What could be more irrational than to allow a brute, a parasitic animal, to interfere with our meals and our conversation?' Not at all points, plainly, was Johnson the typical Englishman we think him. He could not bear dogs; nor, perhaps, anything which interfered with conversation. If he had lived in a Common Room might he not, I wonder, sometimes have been glad, late of an evening, to get away from the conversation of men to that of dogs? I do not mean that I do not like clever conversation. But I tire sometimes (for I am old) of men who do not wish to be understood, and of men understood too easily. I like to be able to retire upon the silence of a creature whose whole being is to understand. Most of the dogs that I have had have wanted cleverness. No one of them has wanted understanding. If they have not understood things, they have understood me.

Since I have spoken of Common Rooms, I will enlist, if it can be done, the diligence of my anthologist to hunt a scrap of literature touching the best of Common Rooms, my own. I know no other Common Room which extends its membership to dogs. But so it is; and the history of the thing—could I but recover it—is interesting. Years ago, a handbook of psychology which I was studying, or playing with, gave me, when I came to the chapter on the Sagacity of Animals, a reference to some periodical of the eighteenth century—I had thought it was the *Gentleman's Magazine*—where there was to be found an article entitled *The Merton Dogs*. I hunted the article out; but where I found it I cannot now remember. But it cannot have been in the *Gentleman's Magazine*, for the good and full index of that periodical knows nothing of it. But what the article told me was something of this kind. Till 1750 (?), Merton, like the other colleges, had no use for dogs in its Common Room. One and all, the fellows kept dogs. But by a self-denying ordinance each don, when he went to his dinner in Common Room, tied his dog up outside. But there came an evening when, between two of the tethered dogs, a difference arose, only to be settled by combat. So deadly was the combat that one of the combatants, wounded so as to move pity in everyone, was taken within, laid before the fire, and tended, resting there till the dons dispersed. And there the matter might have ended. But no. On the very next night there took place yet another combat between two other dogs; and again a dog pitifully injured secured entrance to the Common Room. How many dogs there were in all, I do not remember. But within a short space—two or three weeks—every don's dog, using the same method of appeal, had managed to effect an entrance to Common Room; till, at length, dogs and dons enjoyed equal freedom of membership. Which freedom still subsists—a freedom unknown in other colleges.

These Merton dogs remind me of a Merton dog whom I never saw, and of the sentimental weakness of a great man in whom the last thing that one looked for was sentiment.

I speak of F. H. Bradley, a philosopher of the first rank. Speaking in one of his books of the life of the world to come, there are some of us, Bradley says, who would not much care to enter the kingdom of heaven if it meant leaving our dog outside. He had a dog called 'Crib', a bull-terrier; of which I had, at one time, a photograph. 'Crib's' grave, on the bank of the eastern terrace of the college garden, was, while Bradley lived, graced always with flowers, arranged in six glass tubes sunk in the soil. Till he died, I think none of us knew where these flowers came from, or why they were there. At his death, some of us were told, and, of piety, kept them going; till, one day, an unknowing gardener dug out the vases, disfeaturing the spot. The havoc was not discovered for some while; and then to begin again seemed idle.

I was always told, but I never verified it, that Bradley had an earlier dog, called 'Pusey'. He was christened, it was said, after the celebrated Dr. Pusey. Dr. Pusey stood for causes with which Bradley had no sympathy. The dog was a dog needing frequent correction, and understood no language save that of vituperation. In the garden and in the High Street Bradley liked to be heard using hard names on 'Pusey'. So, at least, it was said. But I am not sure that it was more than plausible invention.

Bradley belongs among great men; not all of whom, but, as I think, most of whom, have liked dogs. Of great men who did not like dogs I have mentioned already one, Johnson. Johnson did not like talking to dogs. So great a man is entitled to be great in his own way. Johnson shared the secrets of his solitude with a *cat*. Ursa Major hugging a cat—it is a queer piece of decadence! But he gets away with it; in this, or in any posture, an appealing figure.

Macaulay is said to have disliked dogs for the same reason as Johnson—they 'spoilt conversation'. 'Seriously to make friends of dogs is not to my taste', he writes. His biographer records, none the less, that he 'was very kind to the only dog which ever depended on him for kindness; a very pretty and very small Mexican spaniel that belonged to one of his nieces. He treated the little animal exactly as he treated children, bringing it presents from the toy-shops, and making rhymes about it.'[1]

Another great man who hated dogs was Housman. Writing to his stepmother from Constantinople, 'Turkey', he says, 'is a country where dogs and women are kept in their proper place.... Pampered and obstreperous animals.'[2] A poet—but he hated dogs. He hated them not because they interfered with conversation. But, like women, they had no business to exist. For no better reason it is recorded that upon one occasion he kicked a dog.

Does anybody remember today 'Dog Dent'? It would perhaps be unfair to call him a hater of dogs. But no lover of dogs can love him. I first made his acquaintance from a poem of Byron:

> My humble tenement admits
> All persons in the dress of Gent.,
> From Mr. Hammond to Dog Dent.

The lines are part of an Epistle from Mr. Murray to

[1] Trevelyan, *Life and Letters of Macaulay*, ii. 331–2 (World's Classics edn.).

[2] *Housman, 1897–1936*, by Grant Richards, 1941, p. 109.

Dr. Polidori. Mr. Hammond, Secretary of State for Foreign Affairs, I knew, for he belonged to my own college, and particulars of him may be found in the *D.N.B.* But not a word has the *D.N.B.* about Dog Dent. Yet the evil that he did still lives after him. In 1796 he was the grand champion of the Bill for taxing dogs. The human population of Great Britain he put, in that year, at 10,000,000; the dog population at 2,000,000. His objection to dogs was, not that they interfered with conversation—I think he liked talking—I find him apologizing to the House of Commons for his own prolixity. But his objection to dogs was that they ate too much; they ate the food which should have gone to the poor. What the dog population is today I have no idea. But I know that there are plenty of poor who would rather go hungry than that their dogs should want. But Dog Dent had his way; and may keep his name. That his primary interest was in food-rationing will excuse him with none of us.

I have mentioned Scott. My anthologist will not need that I should remind him of 'Bevis', or of 'Roswal'. Both names are but aliases for Scott's favourite dog, Maida. The least decadent of men, Scott allowed Landseer to paint Maida's portrait. For Maida he made a monument. For Maida's monument Lockhart made a Latin epitaph (with a false quantity in the second line of it!).[1] Who have been the great painters of dogs, I should not like to say. The earliest painted dog that I recall is in Botticelli's 'Tobias and the

[1] See *The Way of a Dog*, by Sir William Beach Thomas, pp. 122–3. For an earlier dog of Scott's, Camp, and for the death and burial of Camp, see ibid., pp. 69–70.

Angel' (Tobias's dog I have never well understood; in the story to which he belongs he is a mere parenthesis; he does nothing, and, unless it were odd that he should be there at all, we should hardly notice him). Titian painted Charles V with his dog. Van Dyck, when he painted Strafford with a dog, had Titian's Charles V (I must suppose) actually in mind. A century later, certainly Reynolds, painting Lord Ludlow and his dog, recalled both Titian and Van Dyck. But for Englishmen, the painter of dogs *par excellence* is Landseer. Excellent engravers have made some of Landseer's dogs familiar household friends. The most famous of them is, I suppose, the sheepdog of 'The Old Shepherd's Chief Mourner', a picture of which Ruskin said that it was 'one of the most perfect poems' of modern times.

But it was not in my mind that my Oxford Book of Dogs should be an illustrated anthology. The dogs of Dickens would bear featuring. Whether there exist drawings of Diogenes, or Merrilees, or the dog of Bill Sykes, I do not know. But these dogs my anthologist will not miss. Even so, he will find his happiest field, I fancy, not in fiction, but in poetry. Without much thinking, especially if he has been thinking of Scott's Bevis, he will recall the Luath of Burns's *Twa Dogs*. I say that, only to add, ashamedly, that somehow the *Twa Dogs* moves me less than it should. The same is true of a poem by a poet whom I am in general (being English) better qualified to appreciate. When I was a child, Wordsworth's *Fidelity* ('A barking sound the shepherd hears . . .') had a place in the school poetry-books. I learned it, so that I could still say, till the other day, large parts of it. But truth to tell, it is not a poem which I have *by heart*. If I am to speak of poems about dogs to which I give my heart, then I must own to three favourites. Two of them belong, indeed, to my favourite poet—for I think myself old enough, by this time, to have favourites among the poets—to indulge, indeed, all kinds of favouritism. *Geist's Grave* and *Kaiser Dead* are poems belonging to Matthew Arnold's last years. They have none of what he—or was it someone else?—called his 'infernal affectations'. For myself, I like even his affectations. But here, not the affectations, but the affections gently lead him on, making him moving and pleasing, till the distinction between prose and poetry ceases to matter very much. Neither poem is nearly so well known as it should be; and I may be forgiven if I set out here entire *Kaiser Dead*:

Kaiser Dead

What, Kaiser dead? The heavy news
Post-haste to Cobham calls the Muse,
From where in Faringford she brews
  The ode sublime,
Or with Pen-bryn's bold bard pursues
  A rival rhyme.

Kai's bracelet tail, Kai's busy feet,
Were known to all the village-street.
'What, poor Kai dead?' say all I meet;
  'A loss indeed!'
O for the croon pathetic, sweet,
  Of Robin's reed!

Six years ago I brought him down,
A baby dog, from London town;
Round his small throat of black and brown
  A ribbon blue,
And vouch'd by glorious renown
  A dachshound true.

His mother, most majestic dame,
Of blood unmix'd, from Potsdam came;
And Kaiser's race we deem'd the same—
  No lineage higher.
And so he bore the imperial name.
  But ah! his sire!

Soon, soon the days conviction bring.
The collie hair, the collie swing,
The tail's indomitable ring,
  The eye's unrest—
The case was clear, a mongrel thing
  Kai stood confest.

But all those virtues which commend
The humbler sort who serve and tend,
Were thine in store, thou faithful friend.
  What sense, what cheer!
To us declining to our end,
  A mate how dear!

For Max, thy brother-dog, began
To flag, and feel his narrowing span.
And cold, besides, his blue blood ran,
  Since, 'gainst the classes,
He heard, of late, the Grand Old Man
  Incite the masses.

Yes, Max and we grow old and sad;
But Kai, a tireless shepherd-lad,
Teeming with plans, alert, and glad
  In work or play,
Like sunshine went and came, and bade
  Live out the day!

Still, still I see the figure smart—
Trophy in mouth, agog to start,
Then, home return'd, once more depart;
  Or prest together
Against thy mistress' loving heart,
  In winter weather.

I see the tail, the bracelet twirl'd,
In moments of disgrace uncurl'd,
Then at a pardoning word re-furl'd,
  A conquering sign;
Crying, 'Come on, and range the world,
  And never pine.'

Thine eye was bright, thy coat it shone;
Thou hadst thine errands, off and on;
In joy thy last morn flew; anon,
  A fit! All's over;
And thou art gone where Geist hath gone,
  And Toss, and Rover.

Poor Max, with downcast, reverent head,
Regards his brother's form outspread;
Full well Max knows the friend is dead
  Whose cordial talk,
And jokes in doggish language said,
  Beguiled his walk.

And Glory, stretch'd at Burwood gate,
Thy passing by doth vainly wait;
And jealous Jock, thy only hate,
  The chiel from Skye,
Lets from his shaggy Highland pate
  Thy memory die.

Well, fetch his graven collar fine,
And rub the steel, and make it shine,
And leave it round thy neck to twine,
  Kai, in thy grave.
There of thy master keep that sign,
  And this plain stave.

So gentle and engaging is this poem that I hardly like to call attention to the malice in which its first stanza concludes. Who knows today, besides myself, who 'Pen-bryn's bold bard' was? Pen-bryn's bold bard was Sir Lewis Morris. In 1883 he published '*Songs Unsung*. By Lewis Morris of Pen-bryn'. Today they are songs unread. But Pen-bryn was the house, outside Carmarthen, where his grandfather had lived and died. The snobbery of the title-page was more than Matthew Arnold (himself something of a snob) could bear. But what pleased Arnold was the suggestion conveyed by 'rival rhyme'. I have read the unread *Songs Unsung*—when I was a youth, most youths read them. And the author of them really was thought to rival Tennyson. Perhaps he did, he alone among contemporaries. But Tennyson hardly liked to be told it.

The third of the three poems which I mentioned comes from a poet more recent, but no longer living, whose verse never, I think, found the recognition which some of it deserved, Mr. St. John Lucas. It is a scholar's poem, sweet, gentle, humane:

My Dog[1]

The curate thinks you have no soul:
  I know that he has none. But you,
Dear friend! whose solemn self-control
  In our four-square familiar pew

Was pattern to my youth—whose bark
  Called me on summer dawns to rove—
Have you gone down into the dark
  Where none is welcome, none may love?

I will not think those good brown eyes
  Have spent their light of truth so soon;
But in some canine Paradise
  Your wraith, I know, rebukes the moon,

And quarters every plain and hill,
  Seeking its master. . . . As for me,
This prayer at least the gods fulfil:
  That when I pass the flood, and see

Old Charon by the Stygian coast
  Take toll of all the shades that land,
Your little, faithful, barking ghost
  May leap to lick my phantom hand.

Somehow or other, the scholars, I fancy, have always been good when writing about their dogs. This pretty scholarship begins with a great scholar-poet of the French

[1] *New Poems*, by St. John Lucas, Constable, 1908, pp. 85–86.

Renaissance, Du Bellay. Du Bellay had a toy dog, Peloton—a mere ball of fur. When Peloton died he gave him for grave a green mound set with lilies and roses, though his prettiness, he says, deserved a richer tomb. He made for him an epitaph of which the elaborated tendernesses would be hard to beat in any literature. I will not say that the poem deserves to be Englished. It deserves not to be, for it deserves not to die. But let my anthologist not forget it. Yet, in general, let him not go too much abroad. The best about dogs he will get at home. Even Peloton is only a toy, and his master toys with him in poetry. If we are happier with our dogs than other nations, it is because we take them seriously. There is no other way.